Cemetery

AF255324

Book

Melbourne

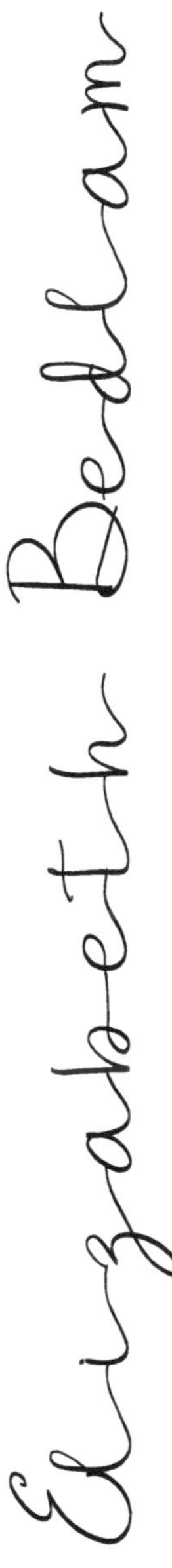

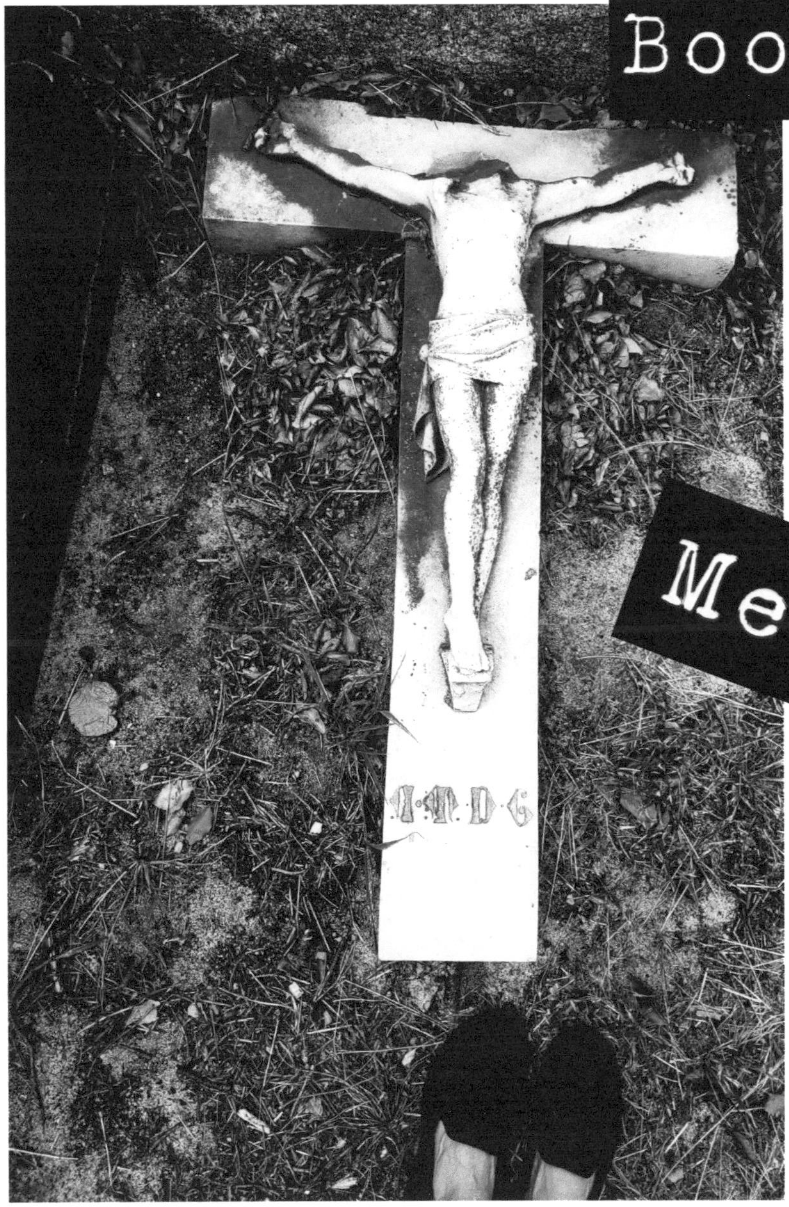

Elizabeth Bedlam

Cover by: Elizabeth Bedlam

Formatting by: Elizabeth Bedlam

All Photos by: Elizabeth Bedlam

Published by: SWANN + BEDLAM 2023

READ THIS ★ DESTROY IT ⚘ Burn it

CUT IT UP AND TAPE IT TO THE WALLS ...SOAK UP BLOOD ....USE TO BALANCE OUT A PIECE OF UNEVEN FURNITURE....

CONTACT ME OR DON'T TO LET ME KNOW HOW IT GOES IF YOU SO DESIRE

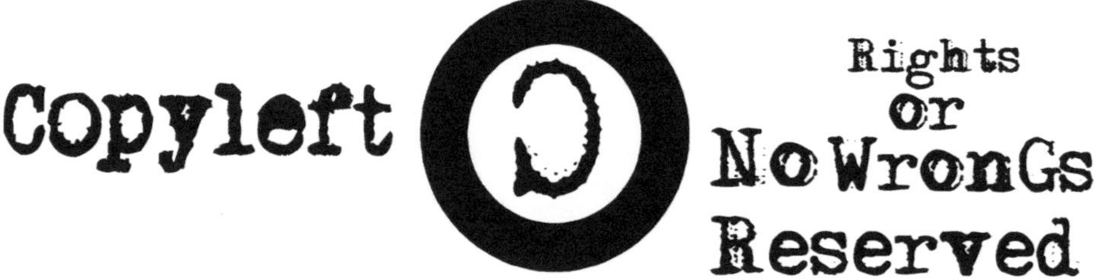

Copyleft Ⓒ Rights or NoWronGs Reserved

Reproduce, photocopy, share....
GIVE TO FRIENDS OR STRANGERS. Feel free to buy extra copies to leave around town... on a bus.... or in a motel room

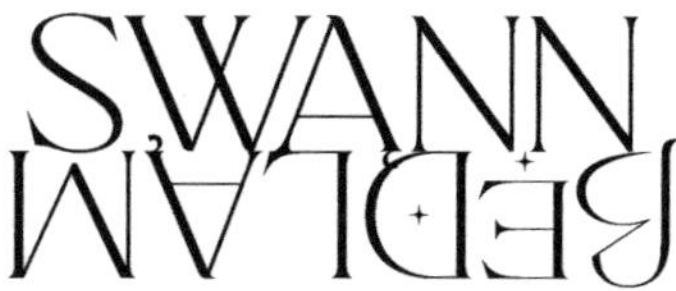

MELBOURNE, OZ
INSTAGRAM: @ELIZABETH.BEDLAM @SWANN.BEDLAM
EMAIL: ELIZABETHBEDLAM@GMAIL.COM
WEBSITE: SWANNBEDLAM.COM

Body of Contents

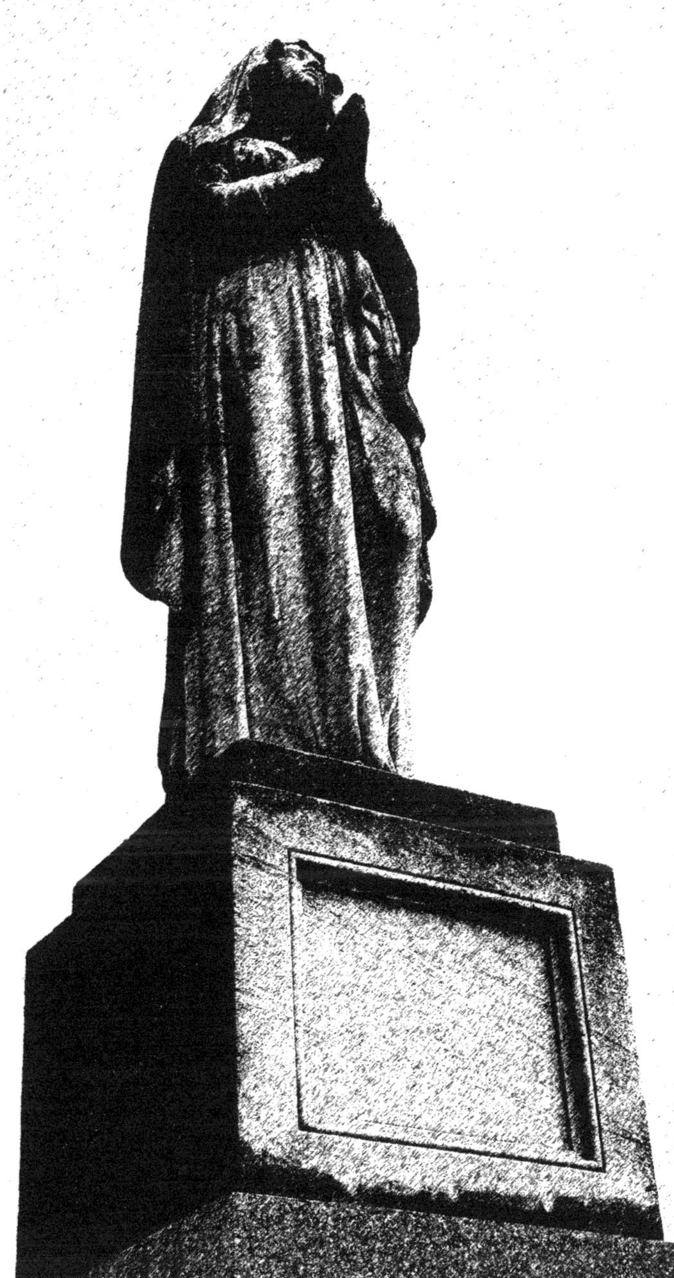

✝ Brighton General Cemetery
✝ Fawkner Memorial Park
✝ Footscray General Cemetery
✝ Melbourne General Cemetery
✝ Preston General Cemetery
✝ St Kilda Cemetery
✝ Williamstown Cemetery

Taphophile: n. A person who is interested in cemeteries, funerals and gravestones

Tombstone Tourist: n. a passion for and enjoyment of cemeteries

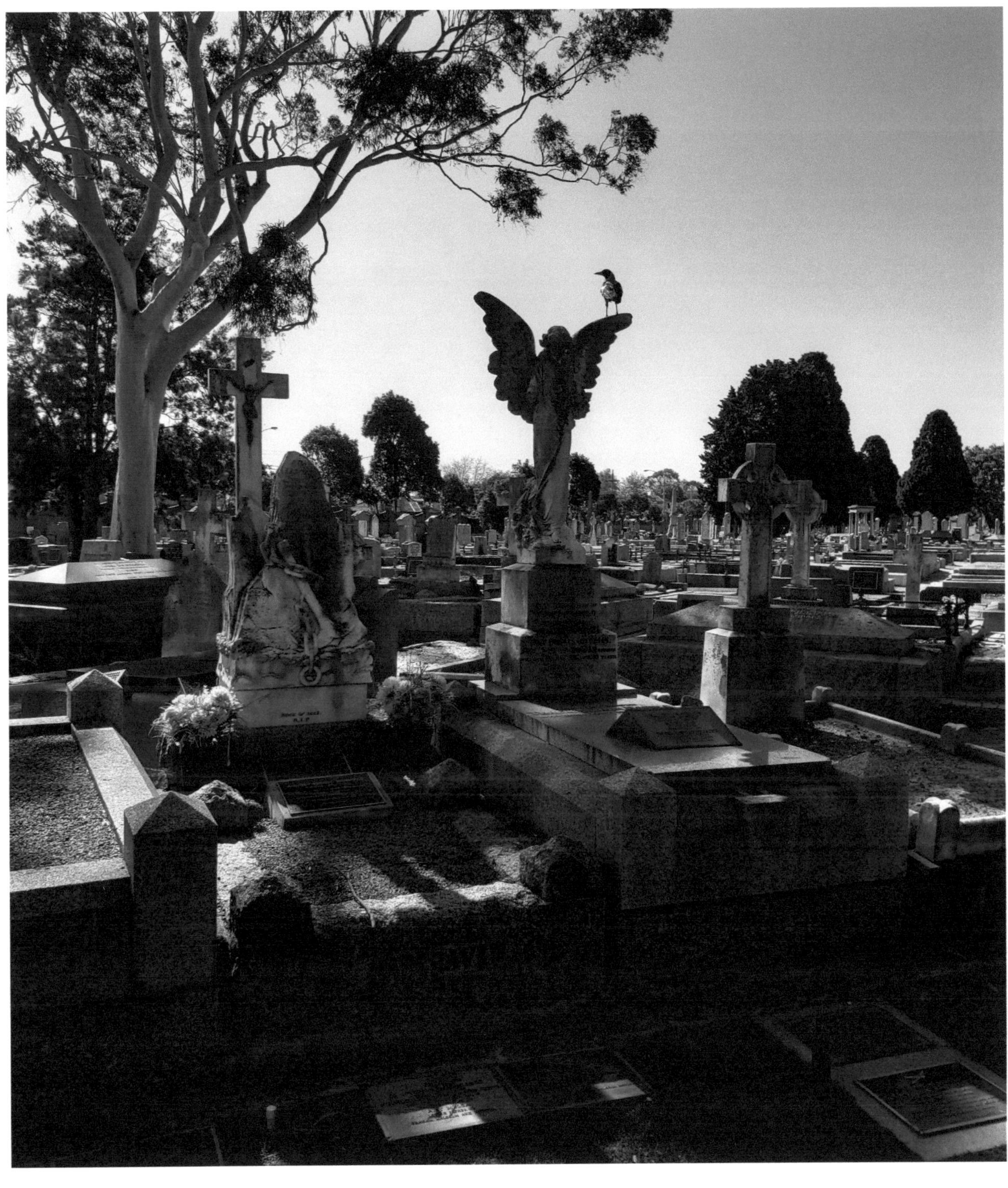

Brighton General Cemetery

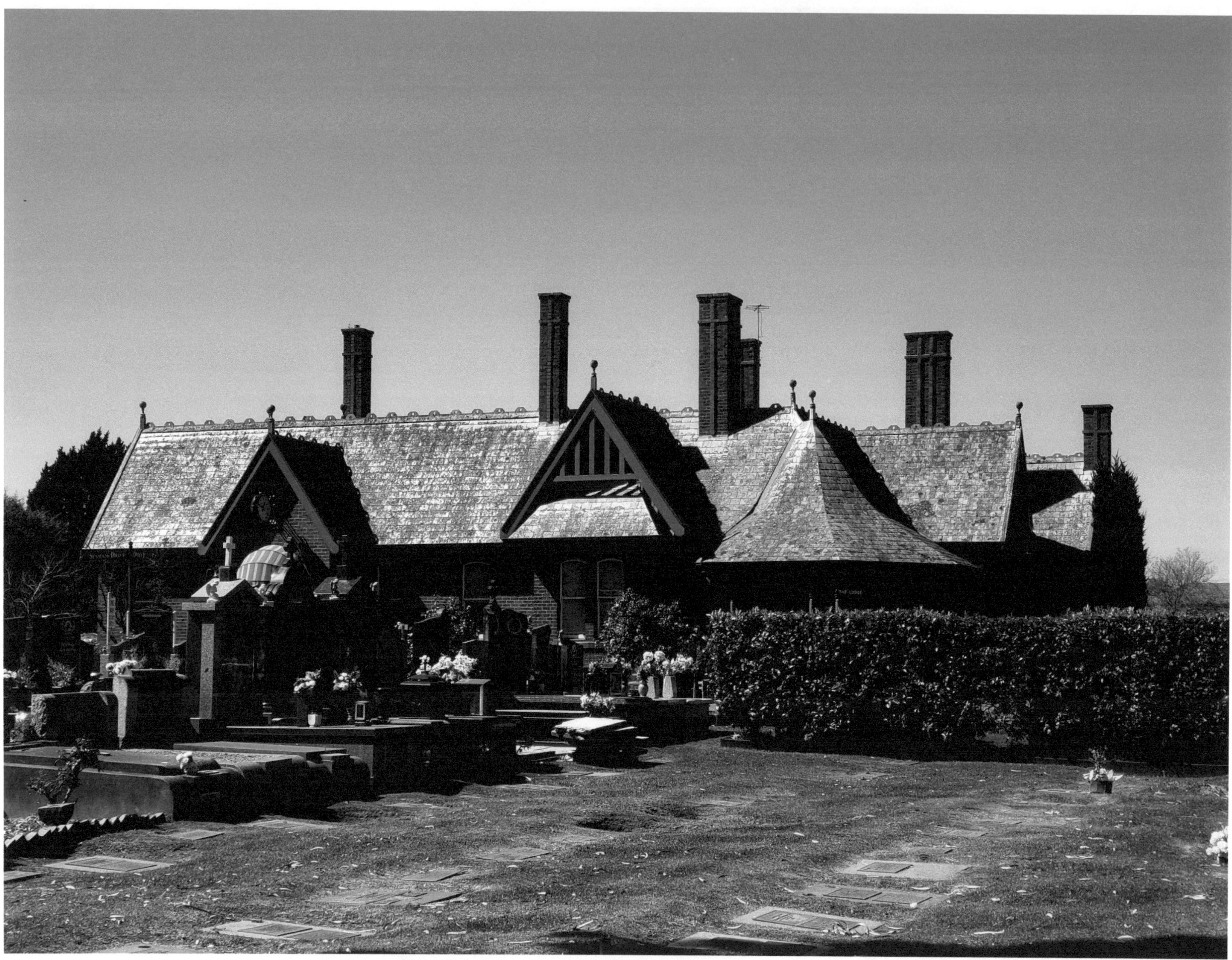

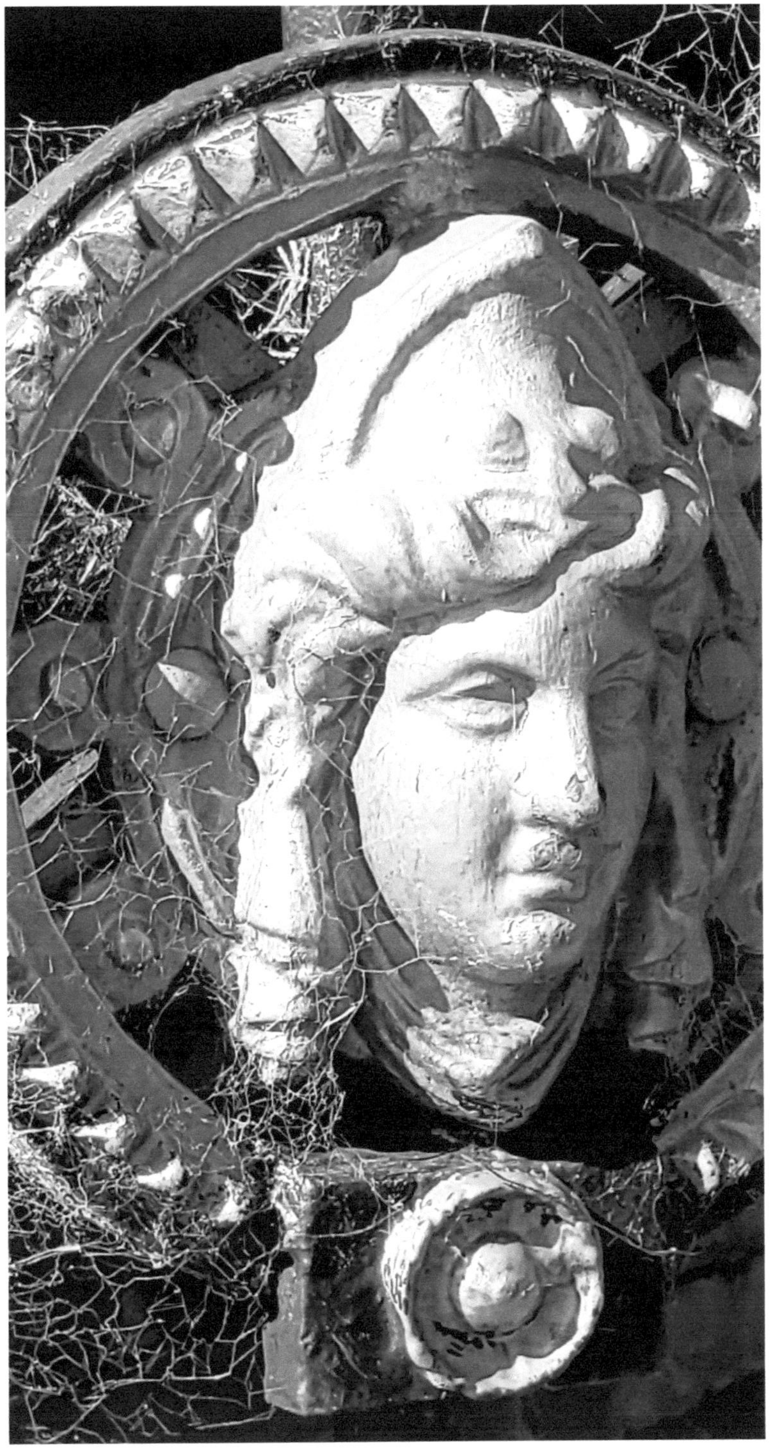

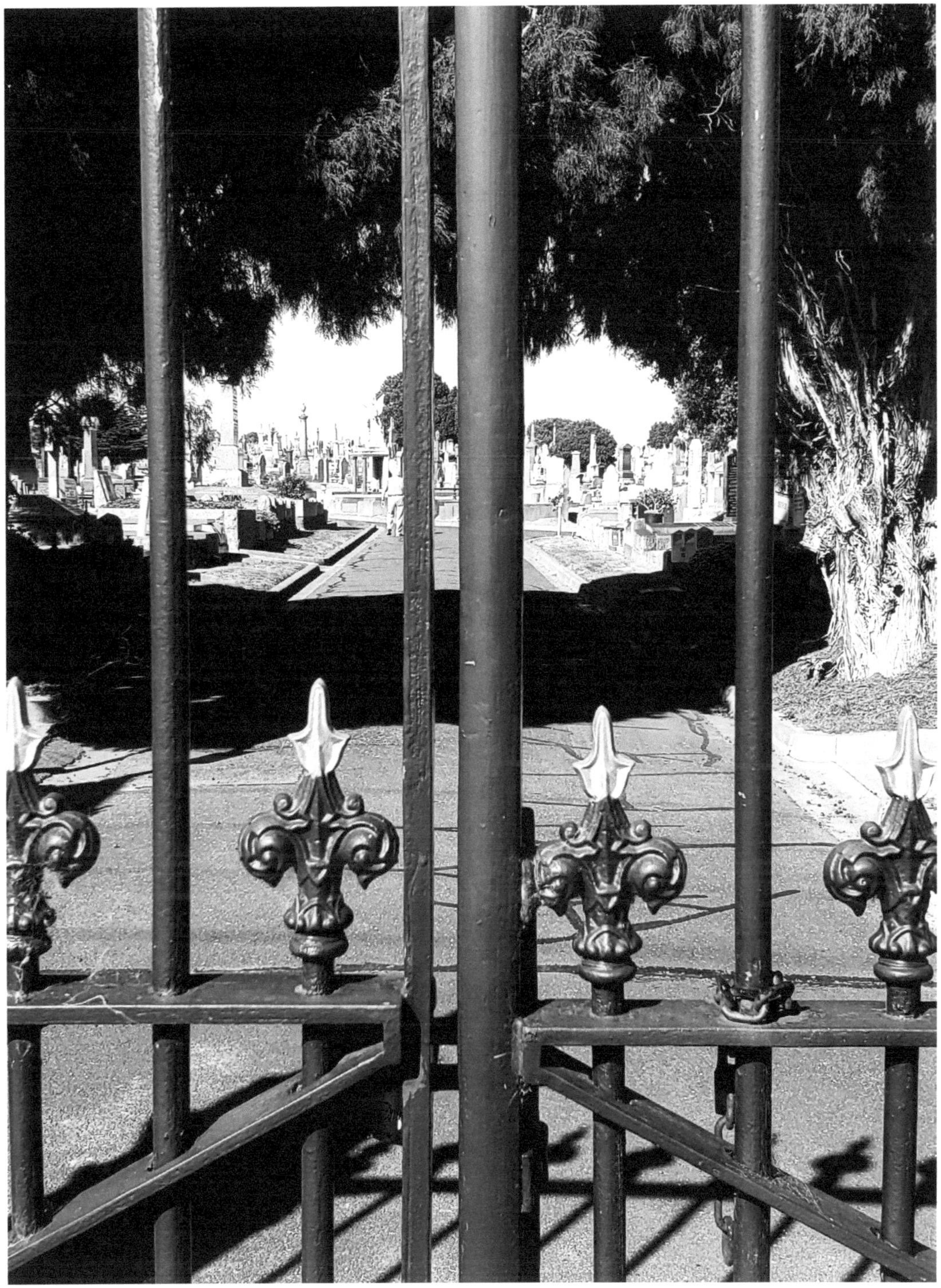

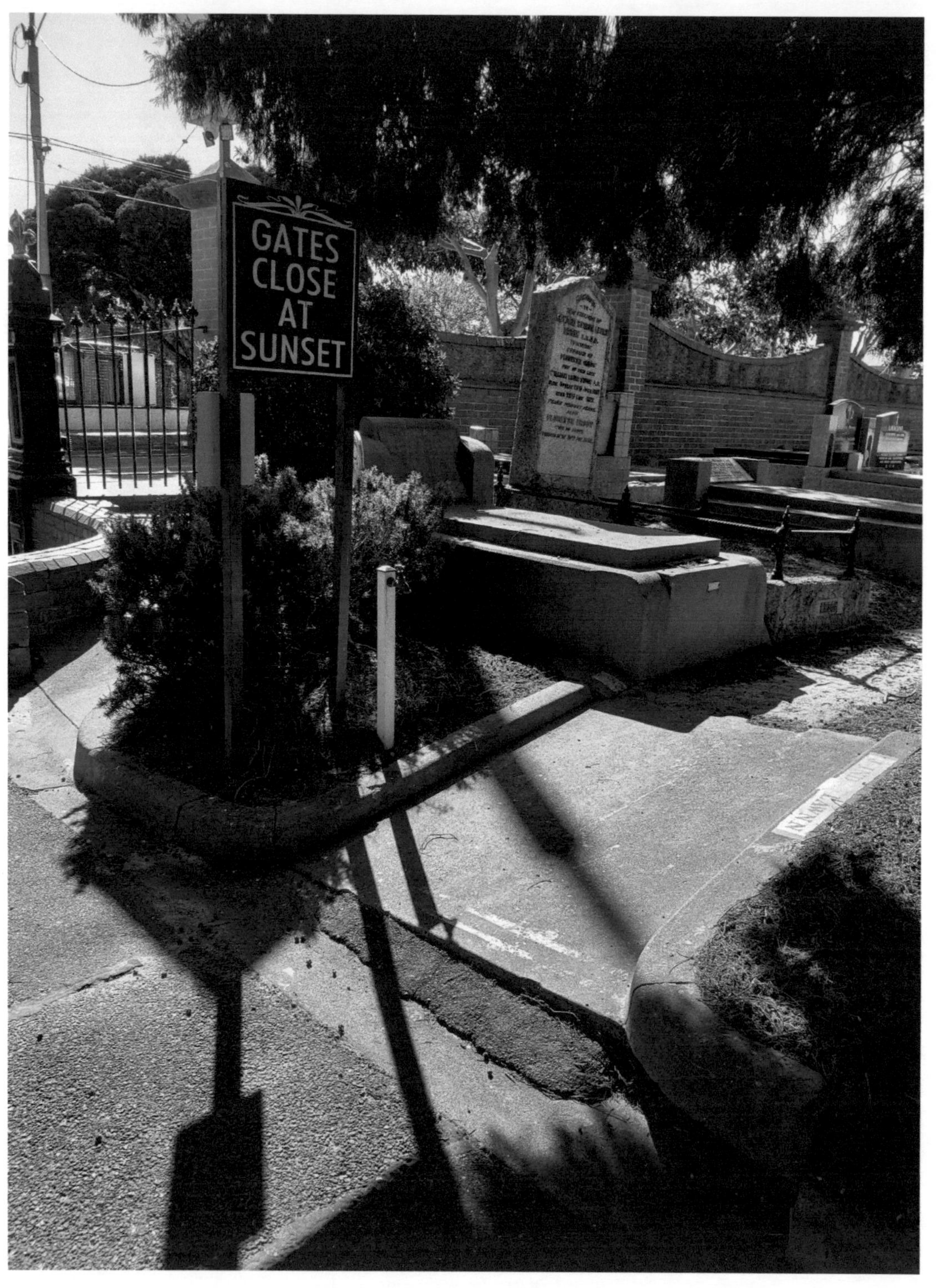
GATES
CLOSE
AT
SUNSET

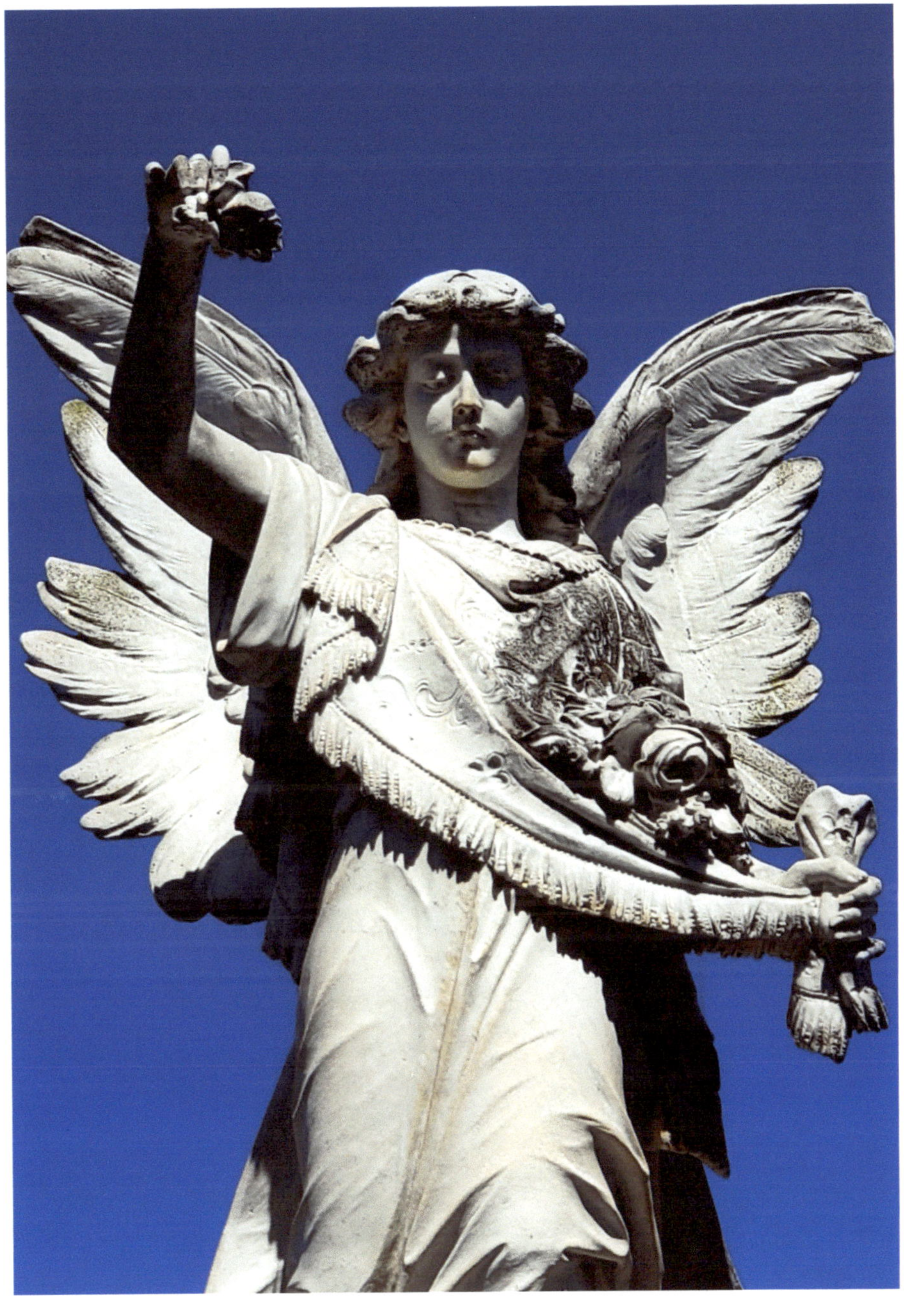

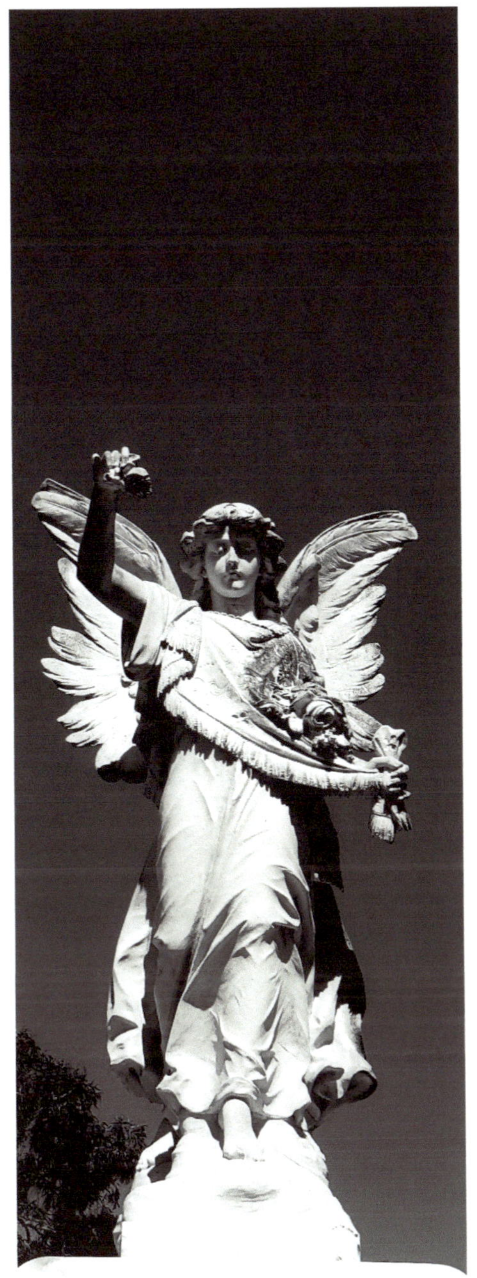
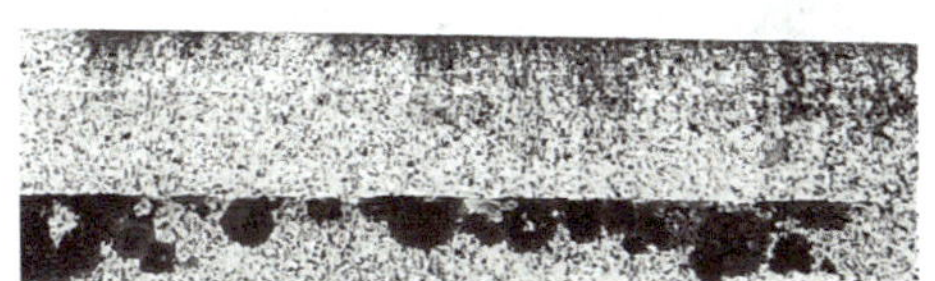
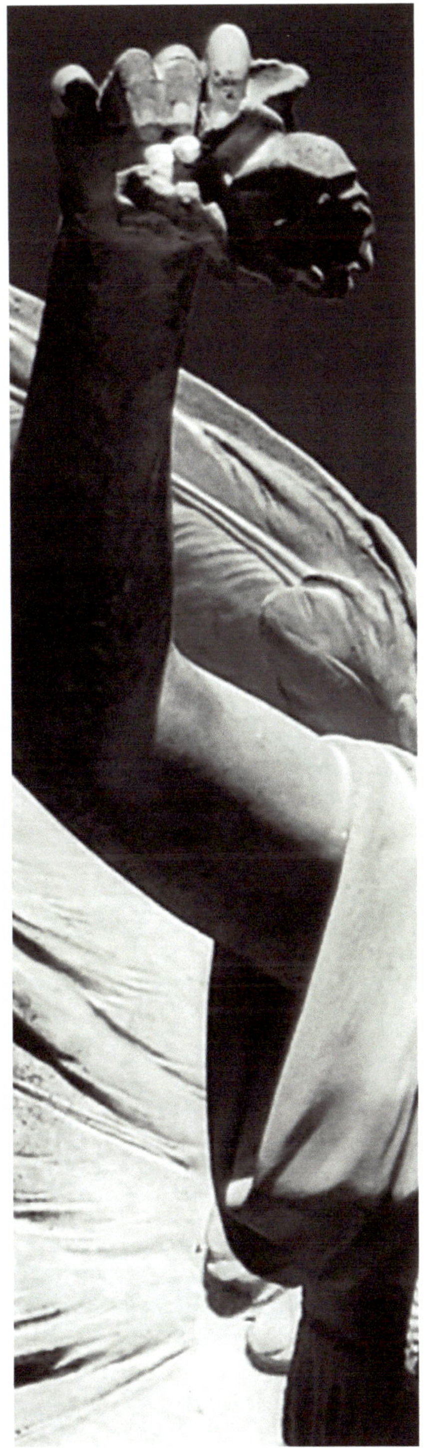

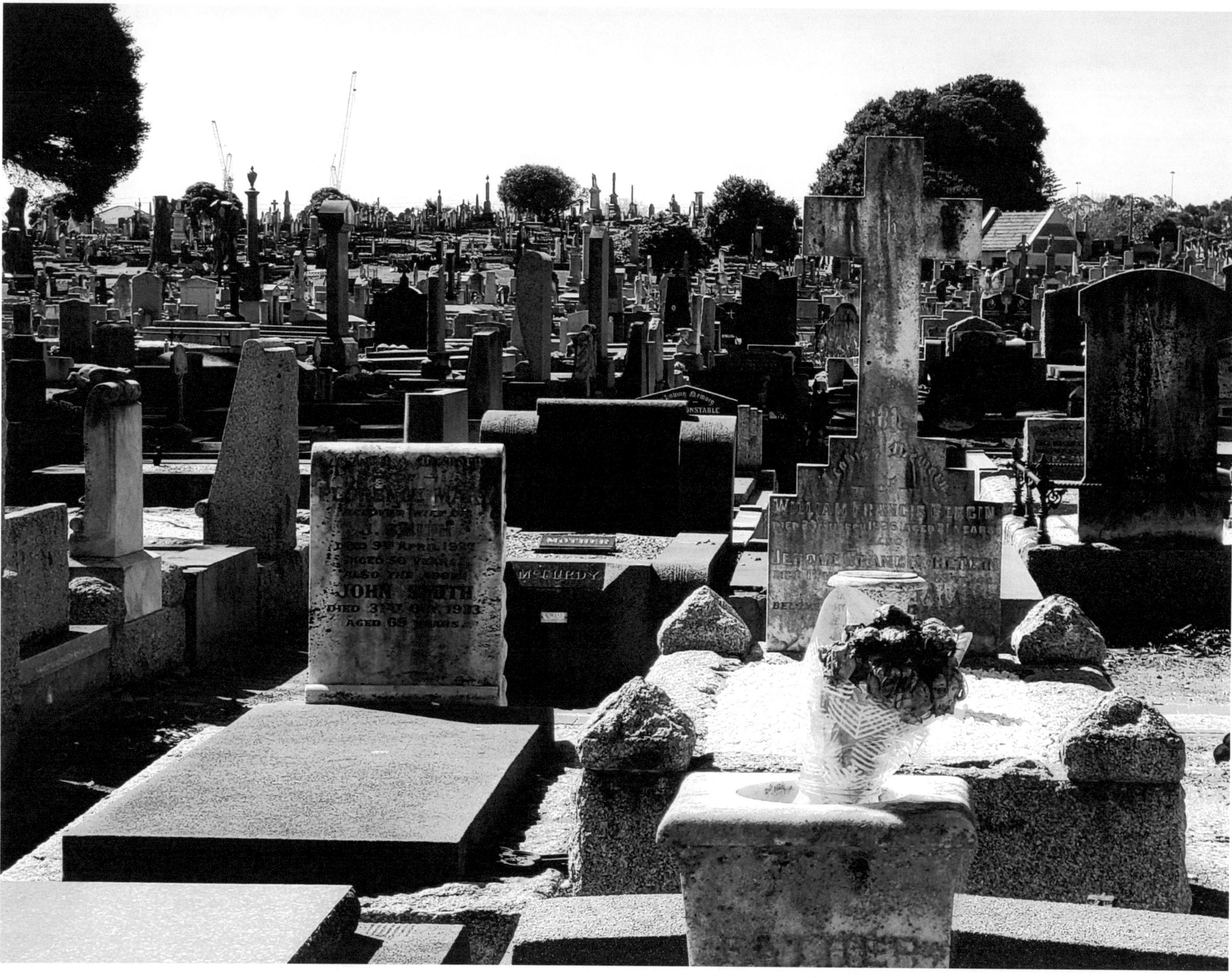
FLORENCE MARY
BELOVED WIFE OF
J. SMITH
DIED 9TH APRIL 1927
AGED 50 YEARS
ALSO THE ABOVE
JOHN SMITH
DIED 31ST OCT 1933
AGED 69 YEARS
MOTHER
McCURDY
WILLIAM FRANCIS BERGIN
JEROME FRANCIS
CONSTABLE

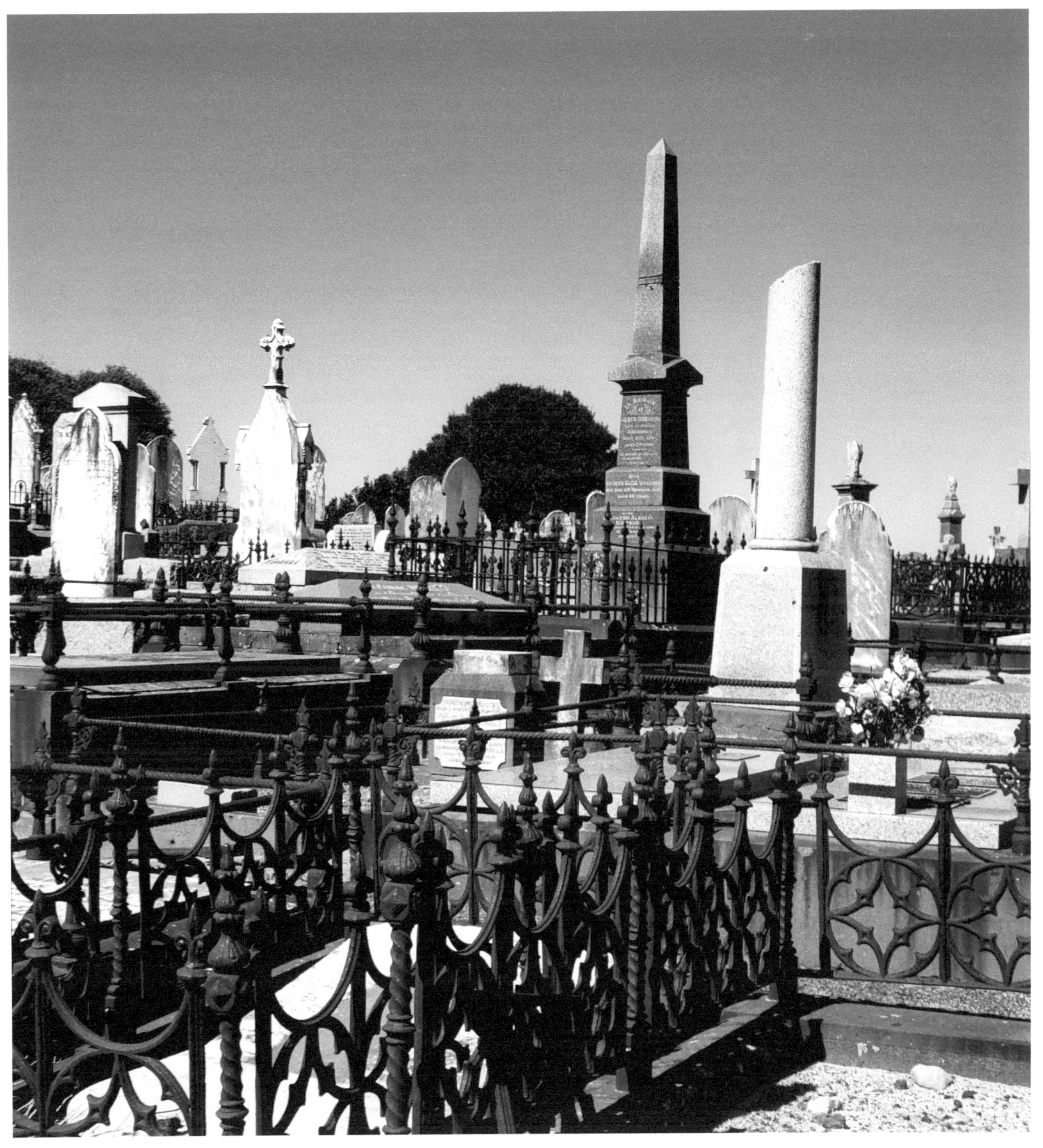

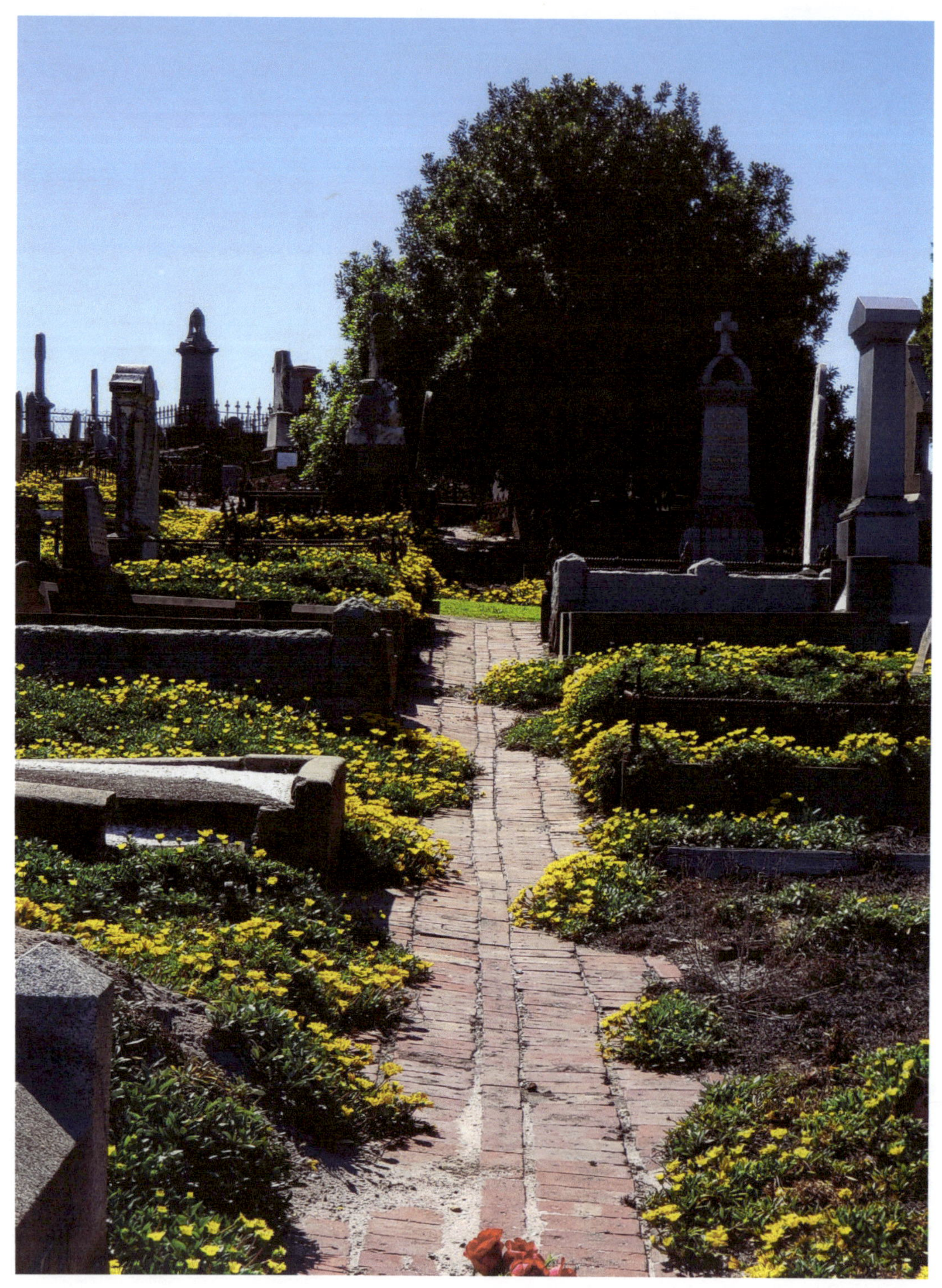

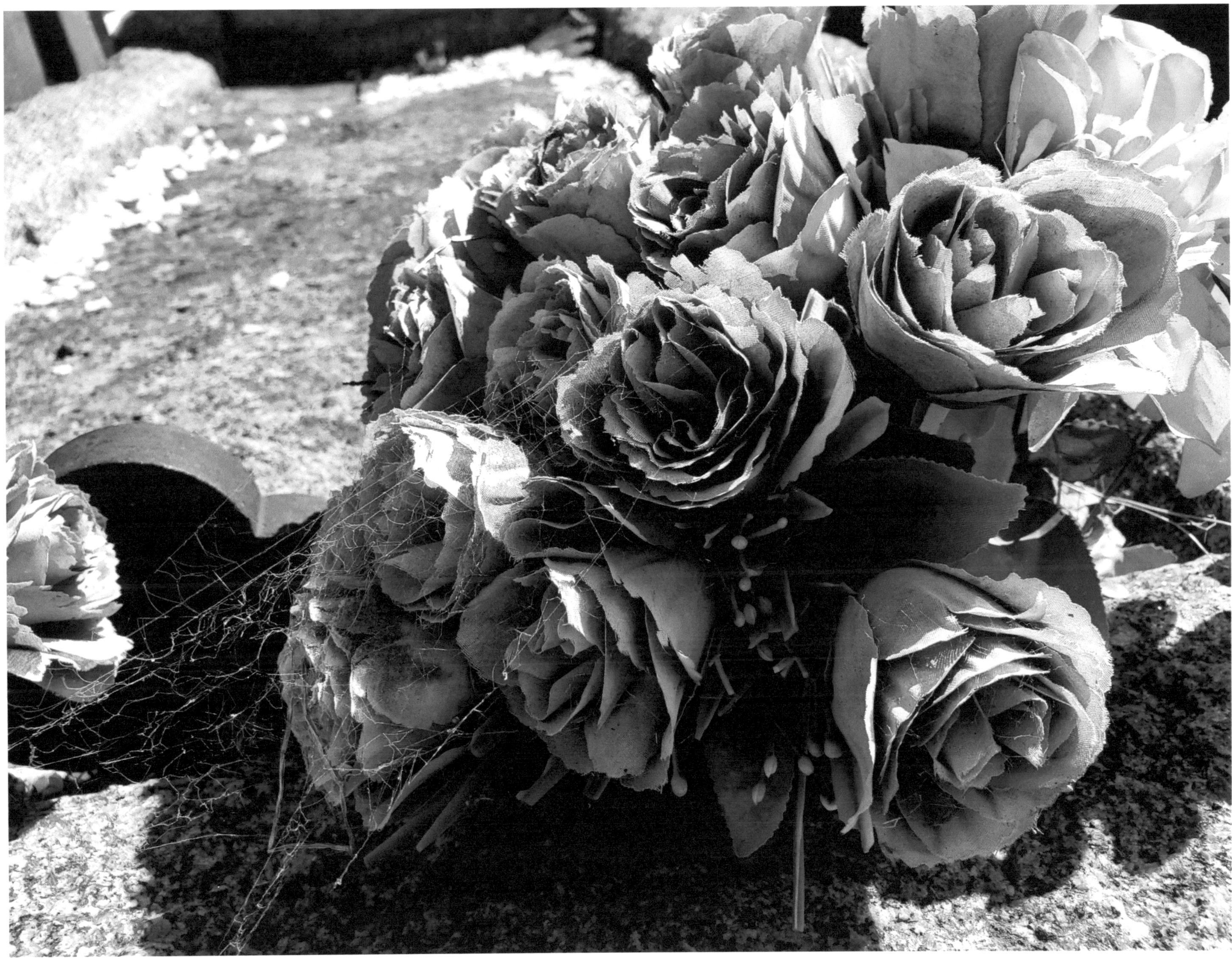

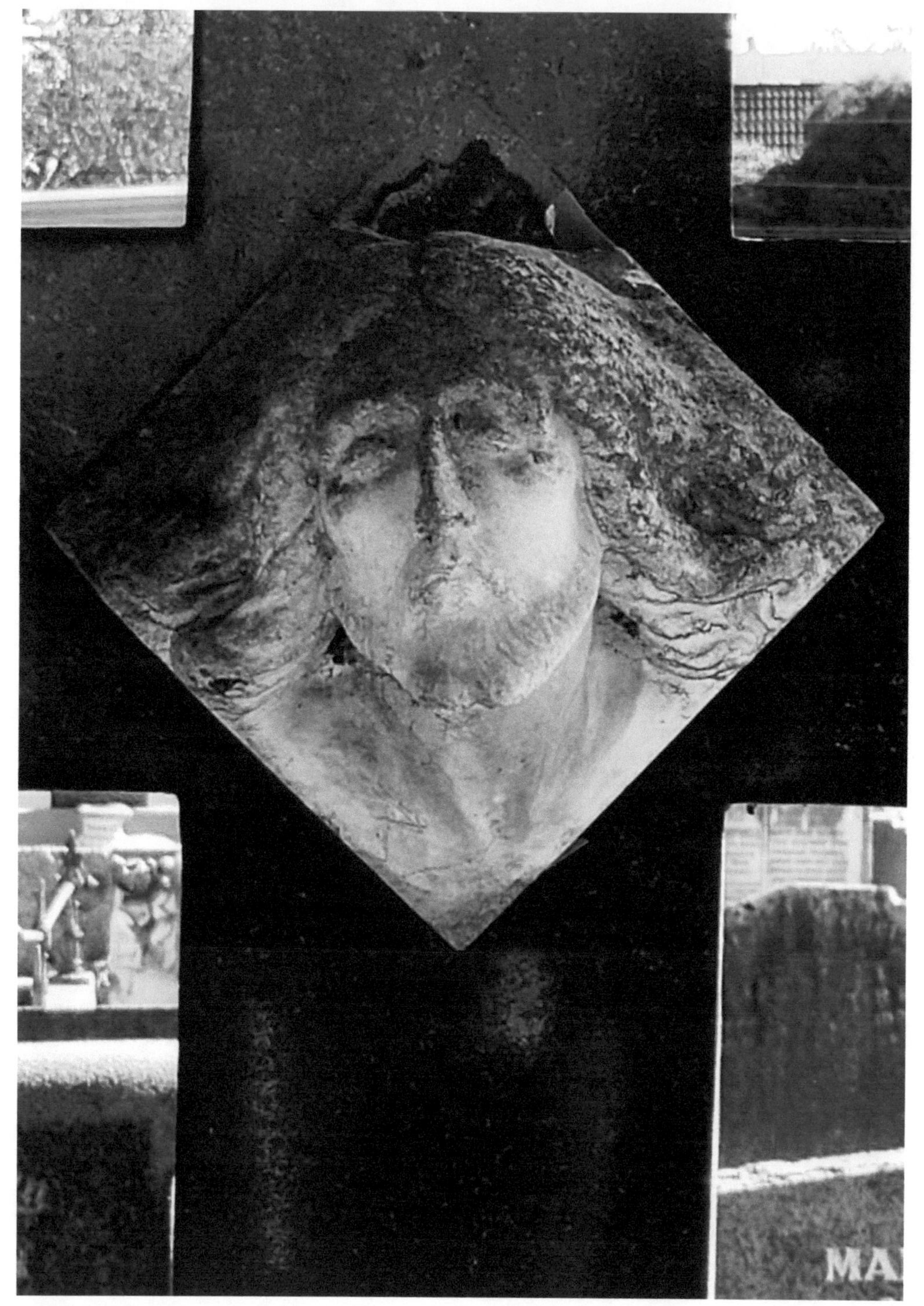

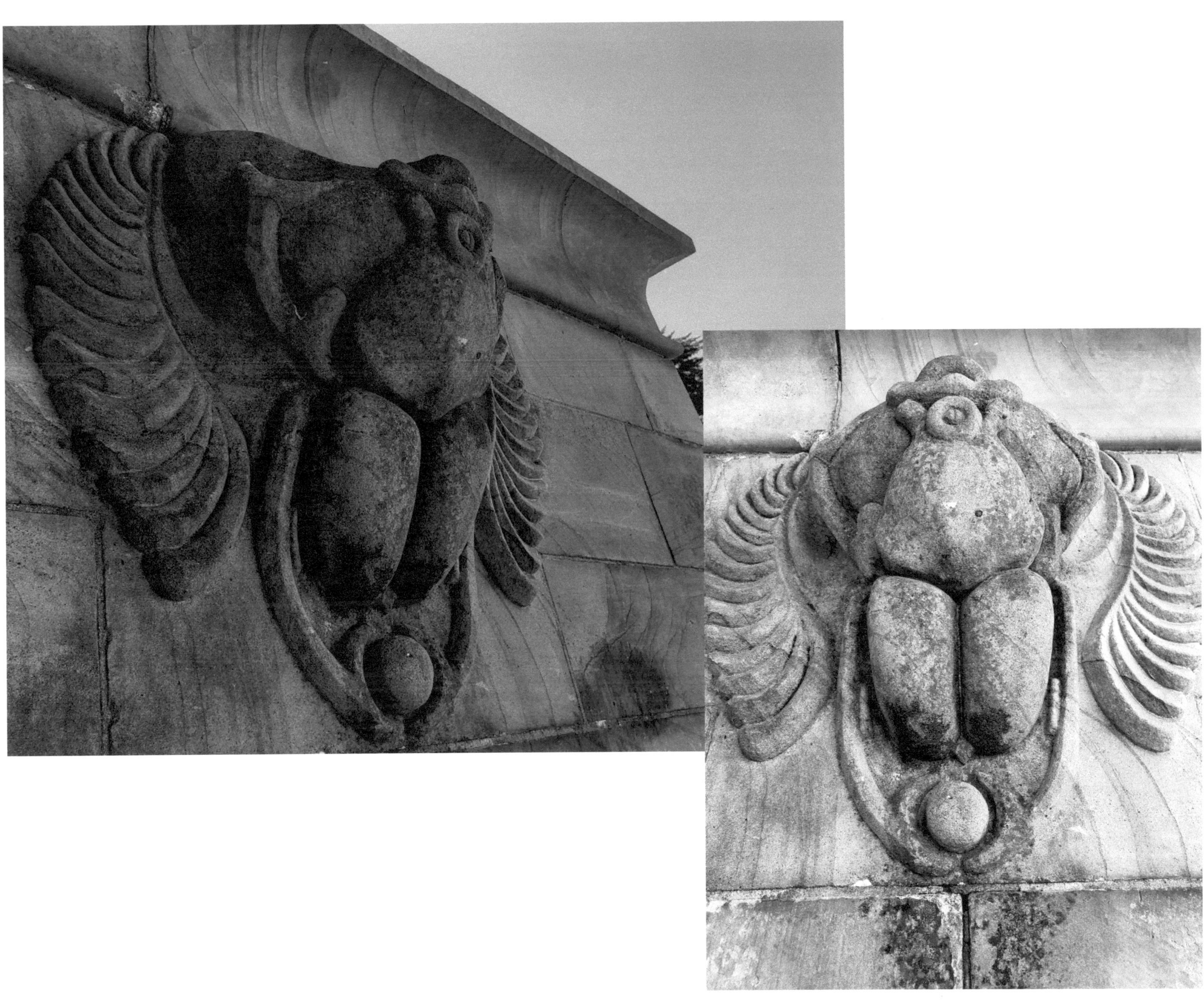

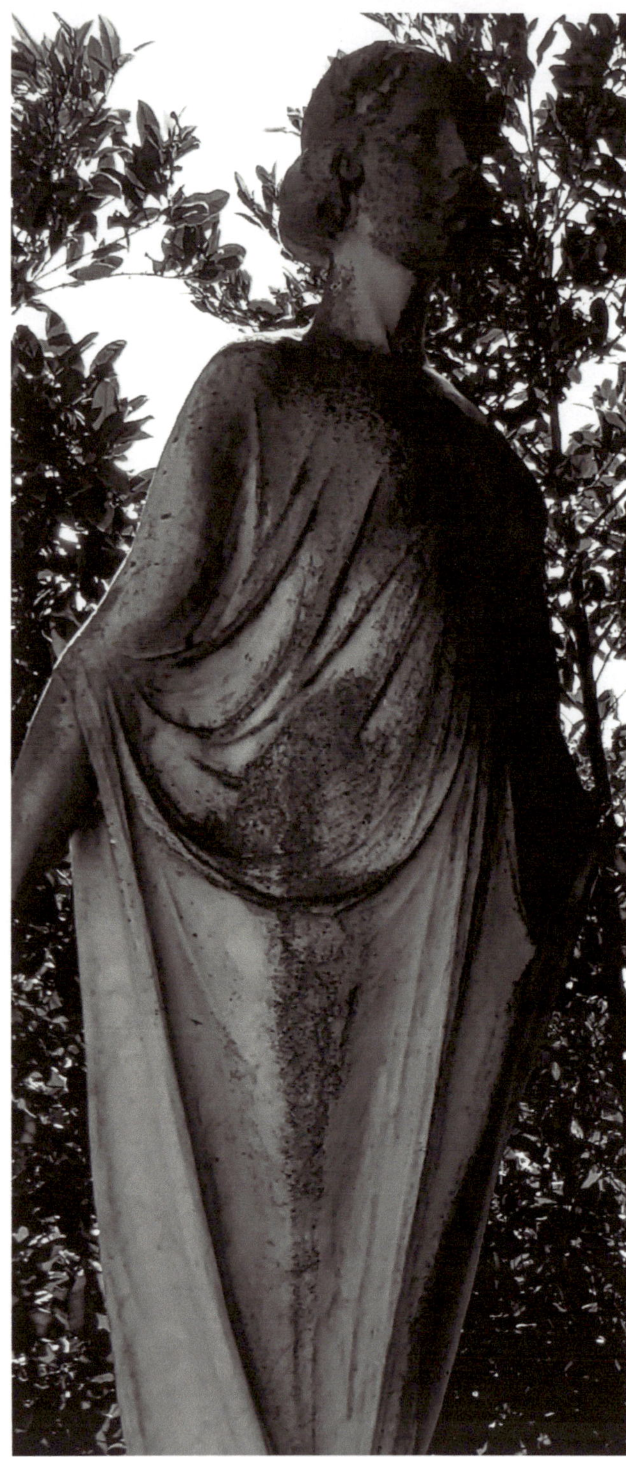
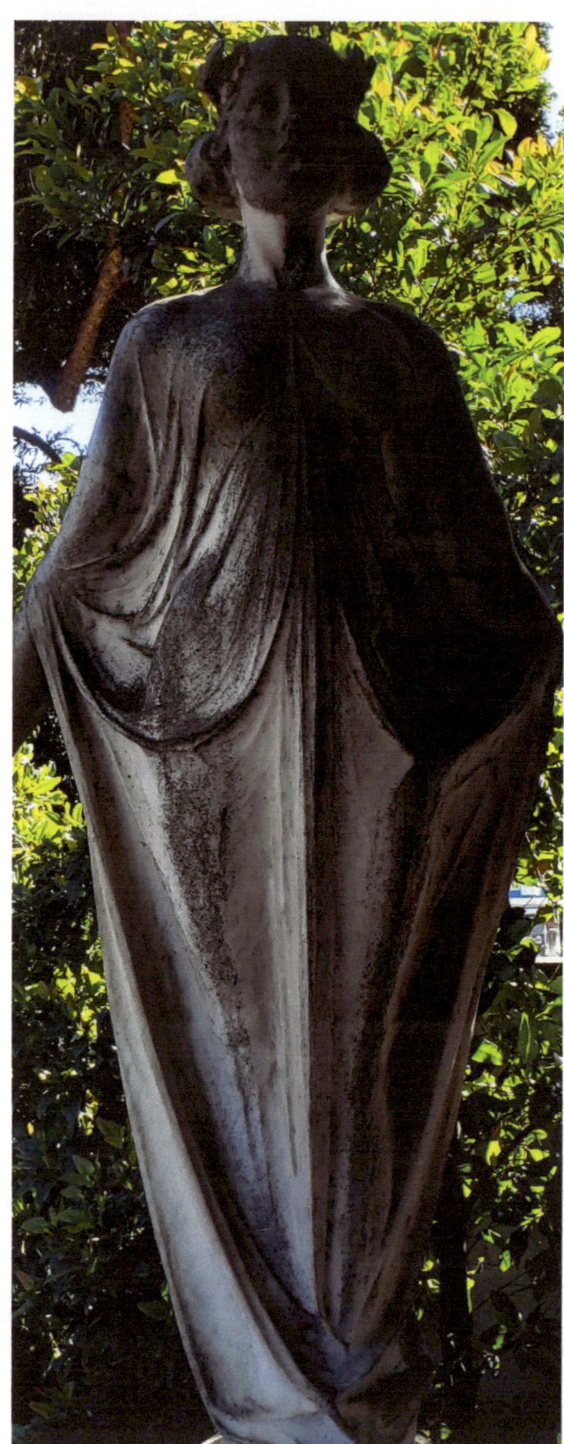
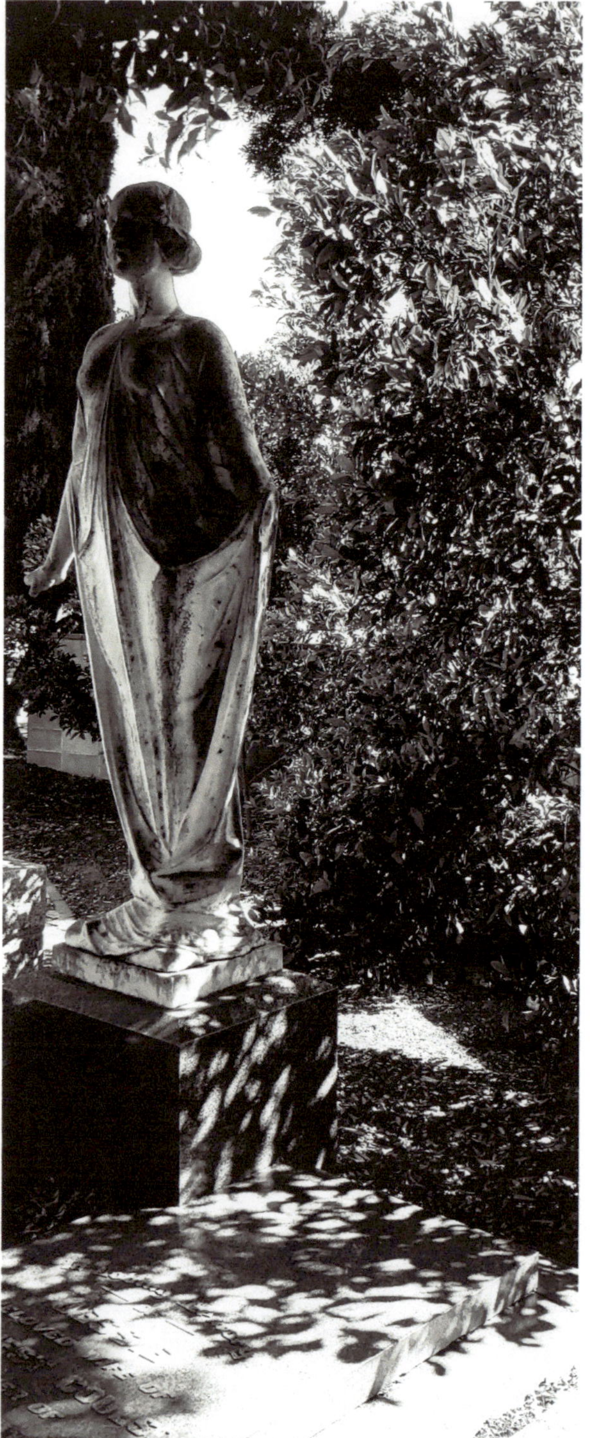

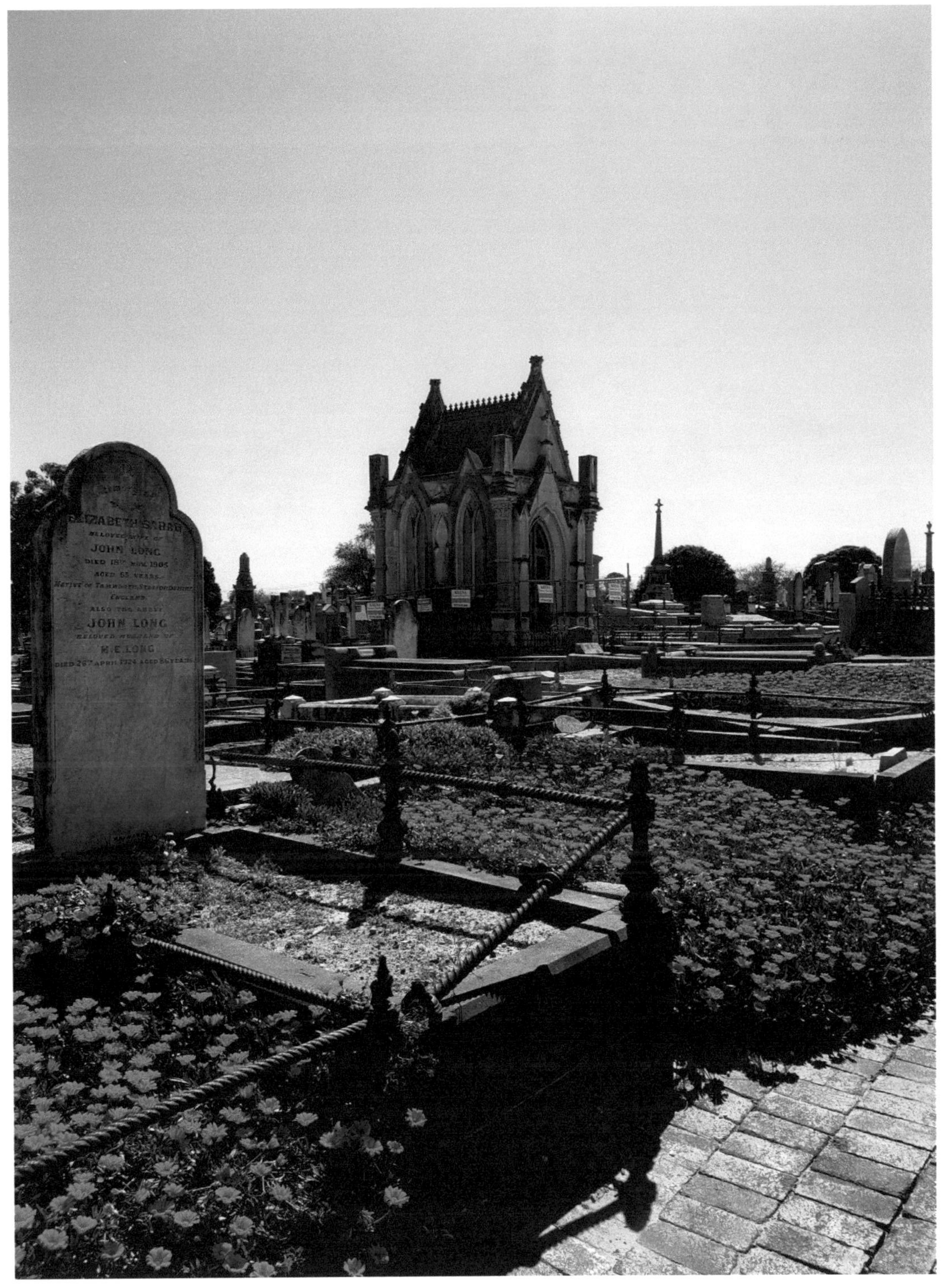

Fawkner Memorial Park

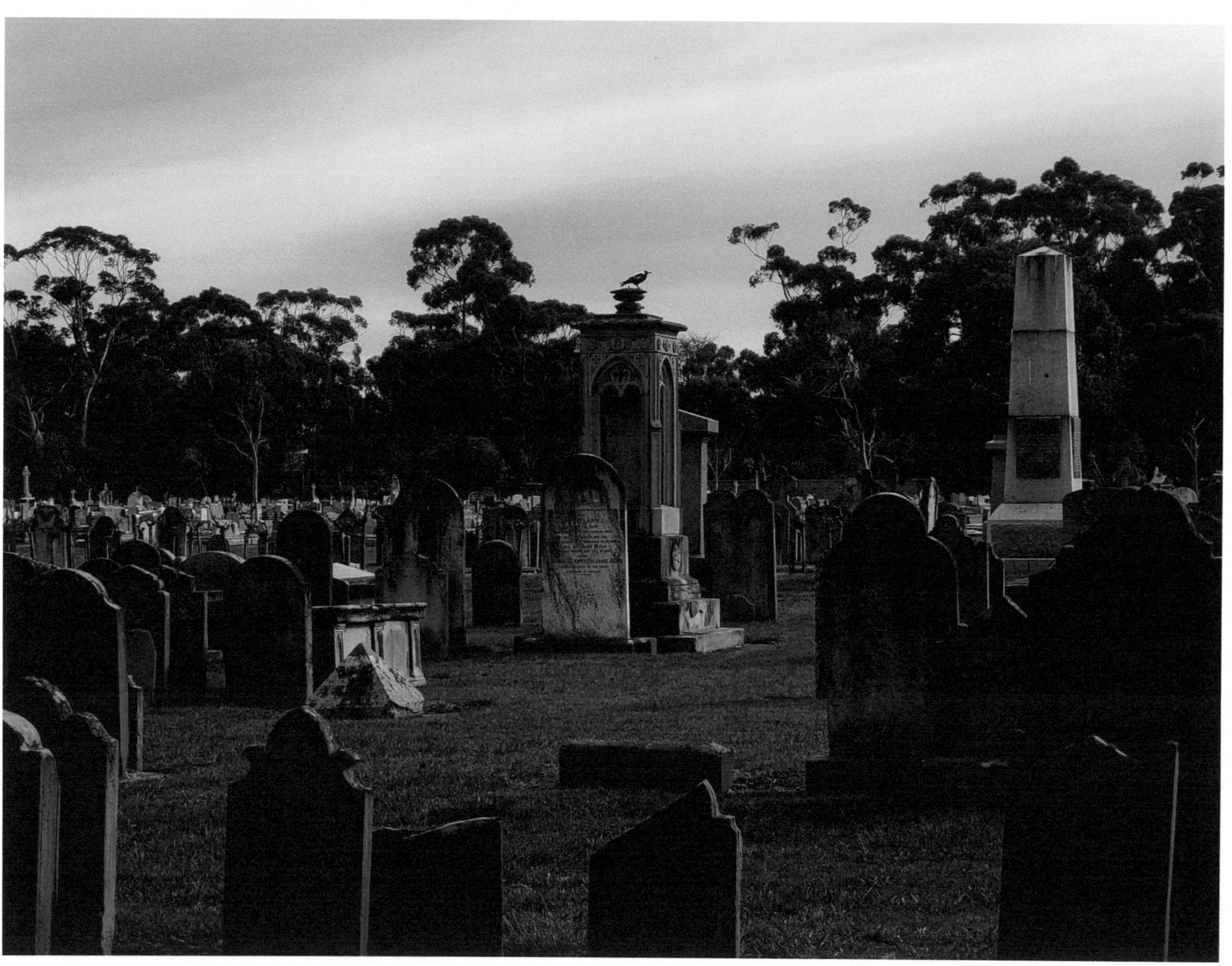

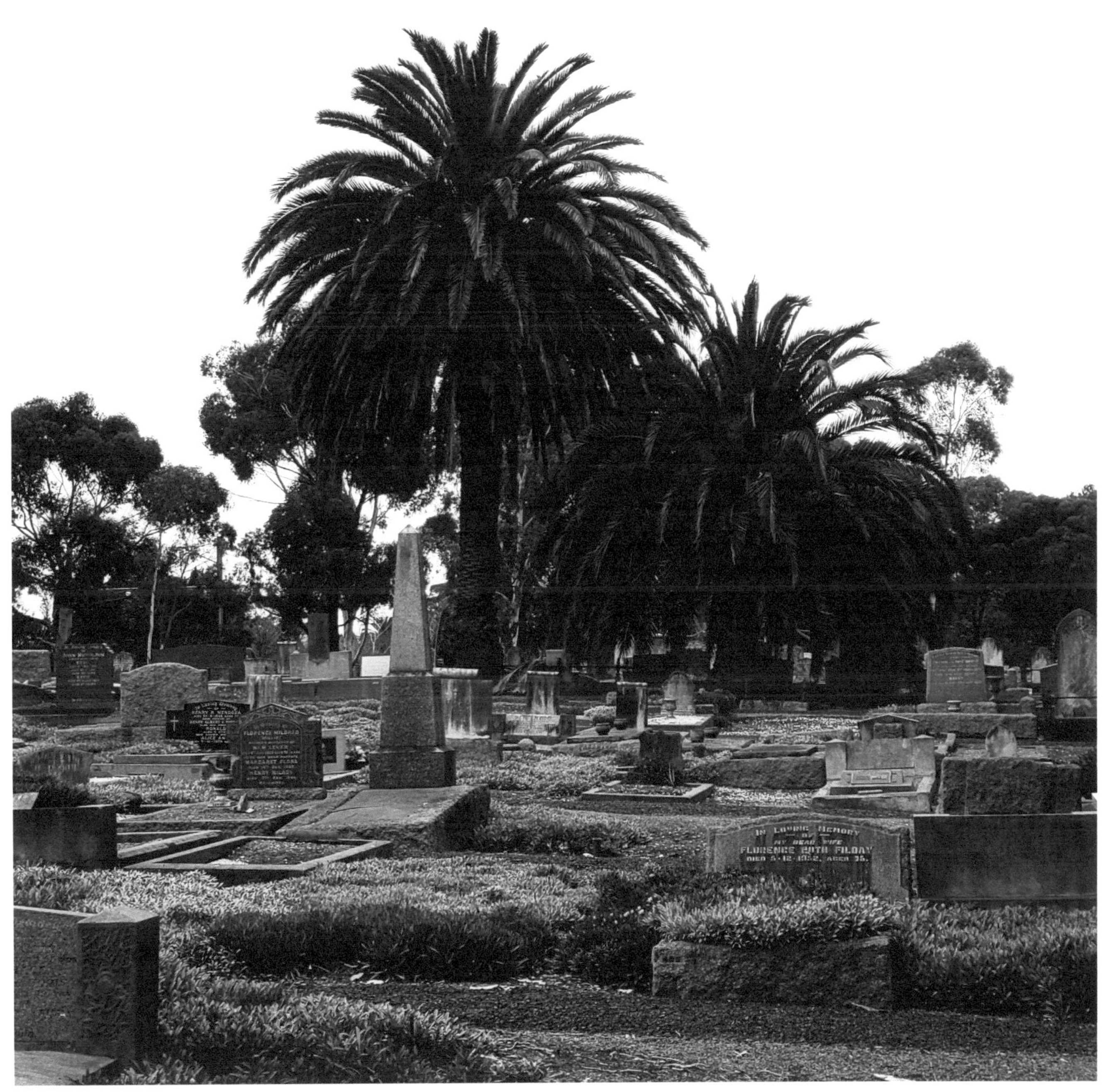

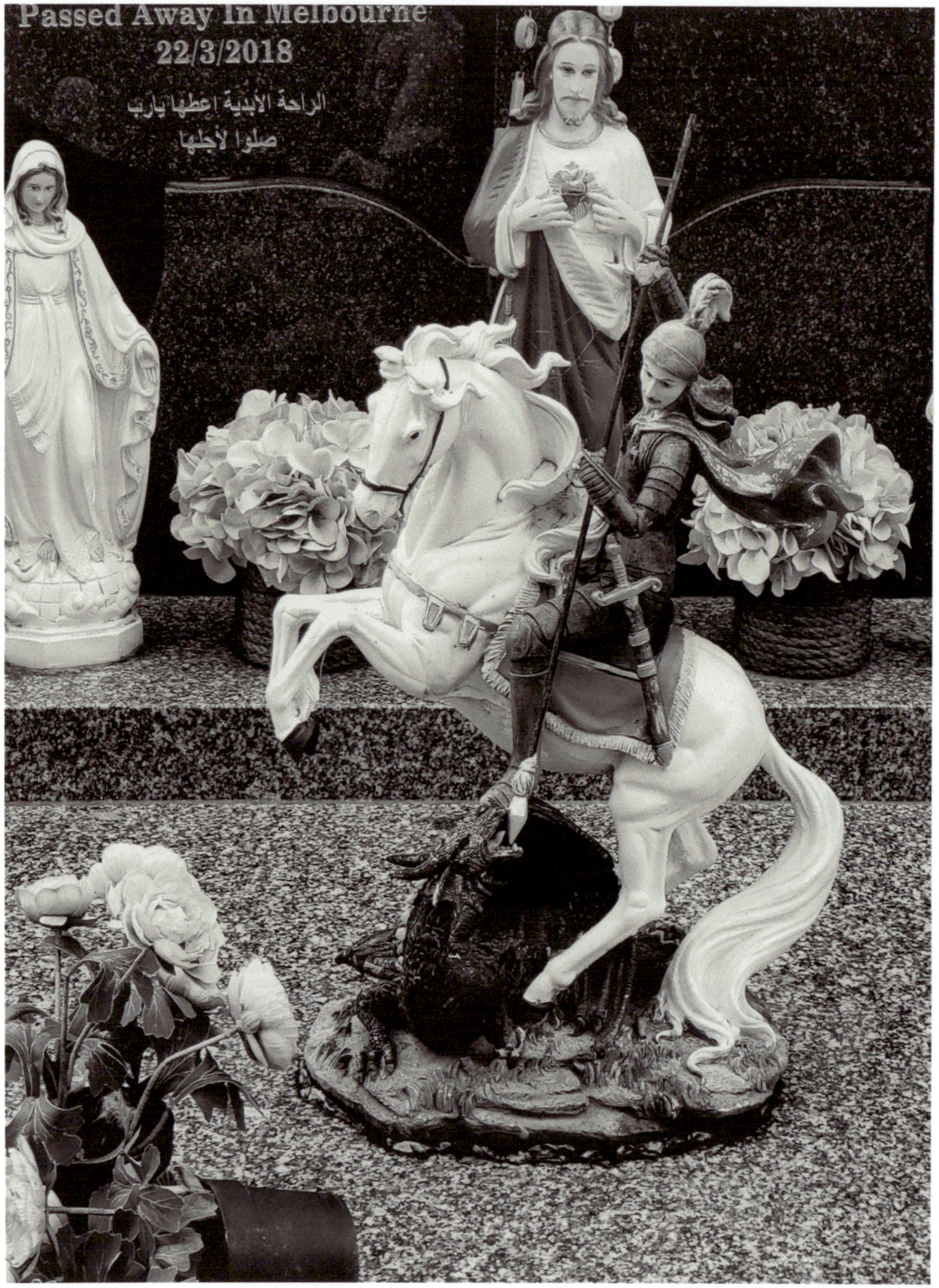

Passed Away In Melbourne
22/3/2018
الراحة الأبدية اعطها يارب
صلوا لأجلها

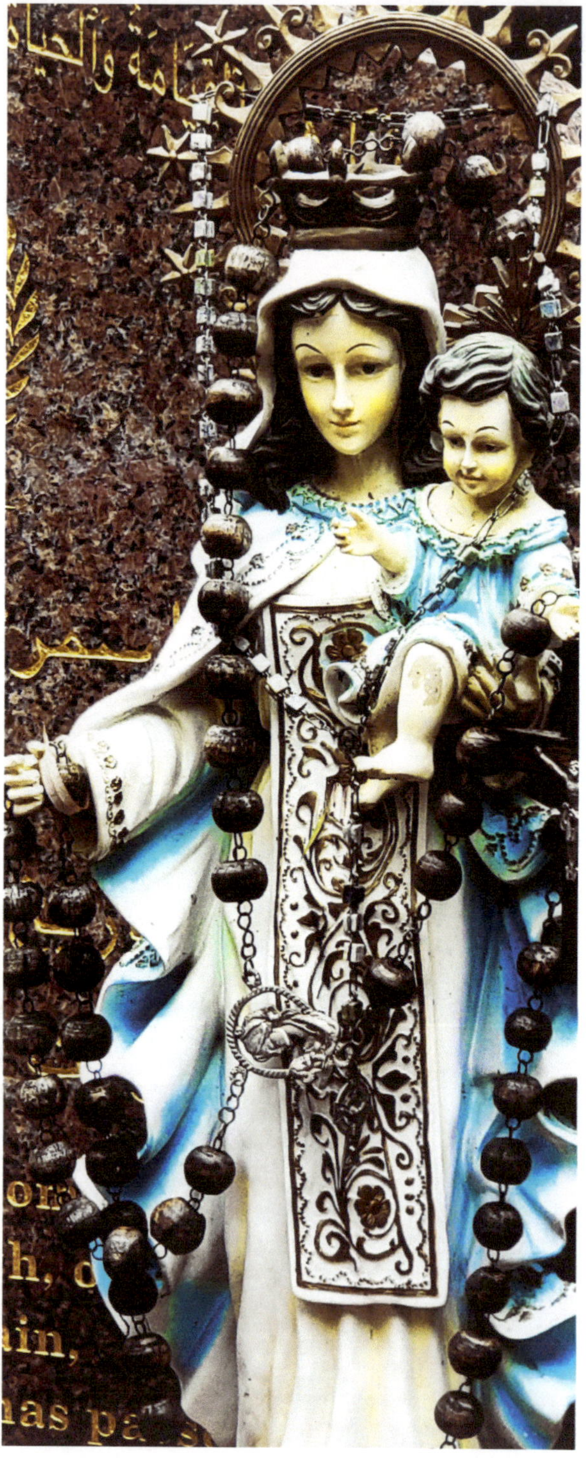

قيامة والحياة

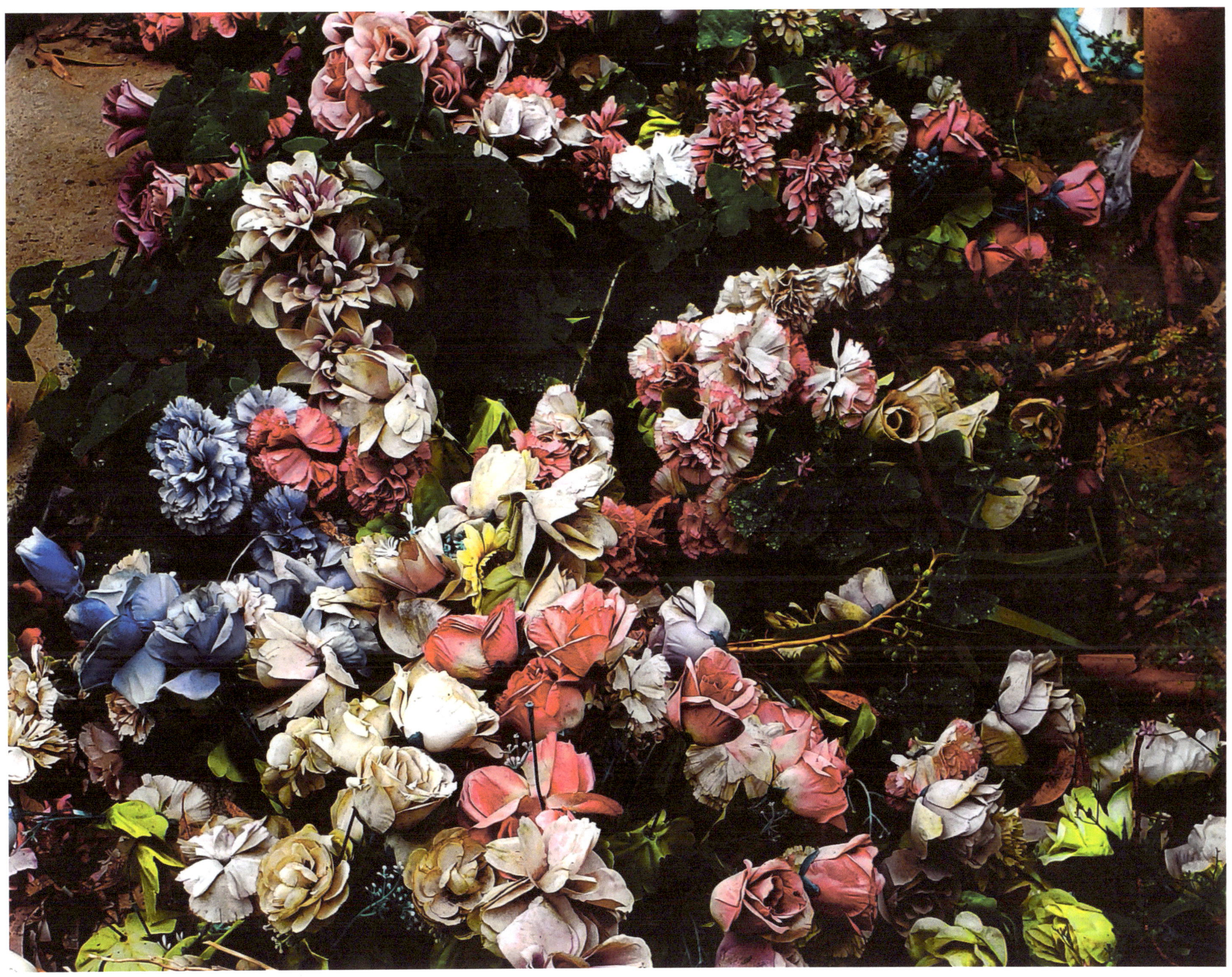

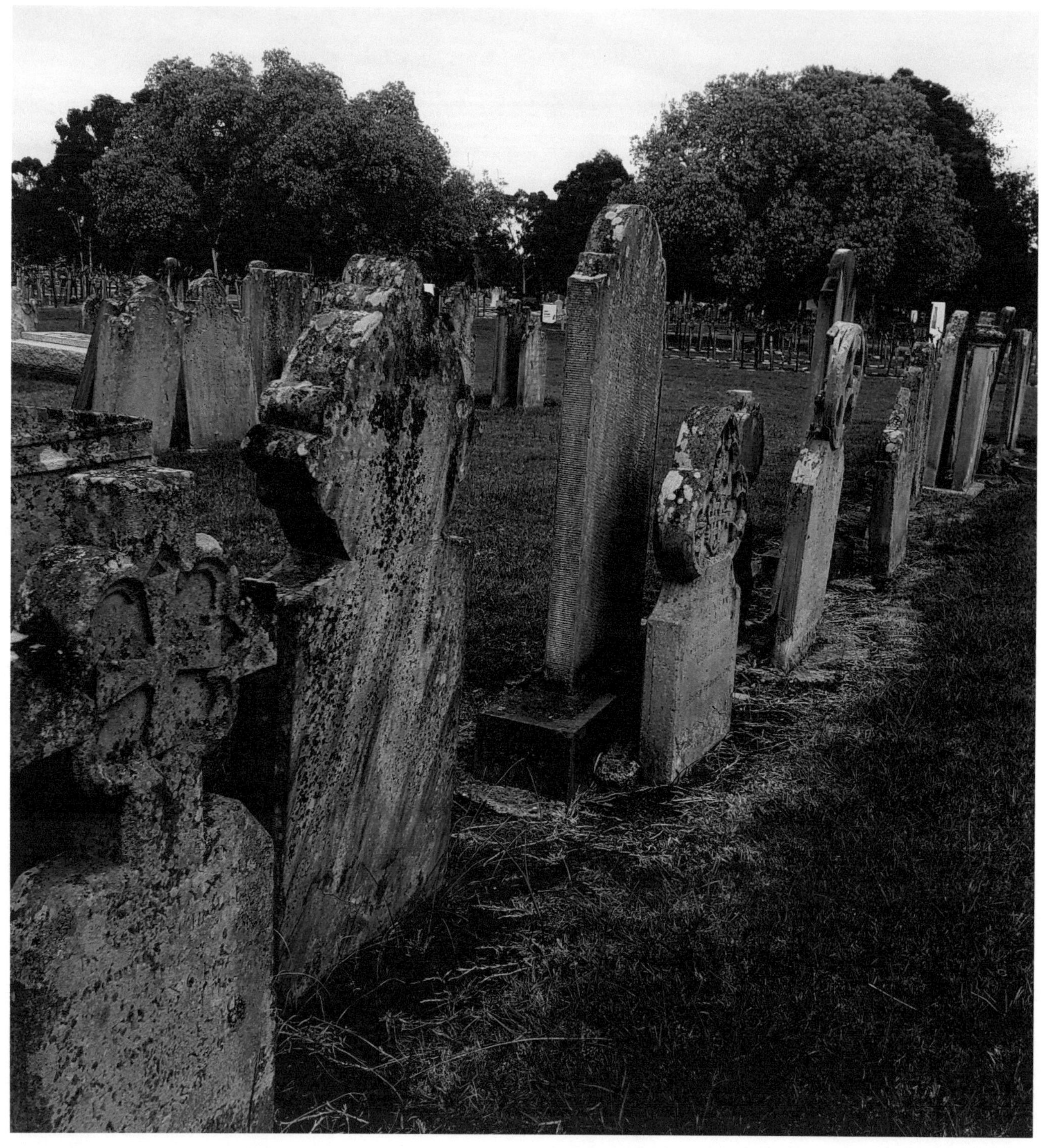

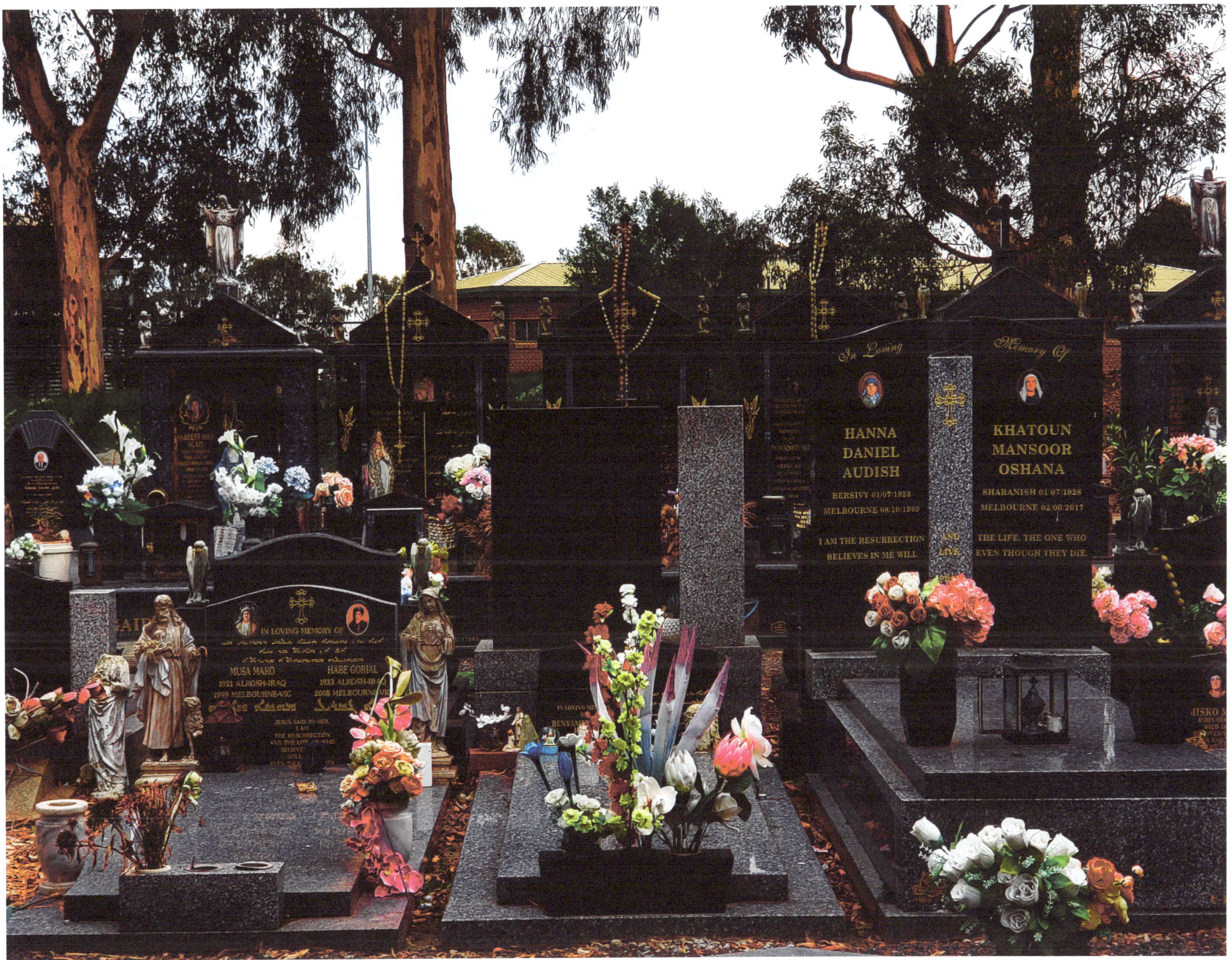

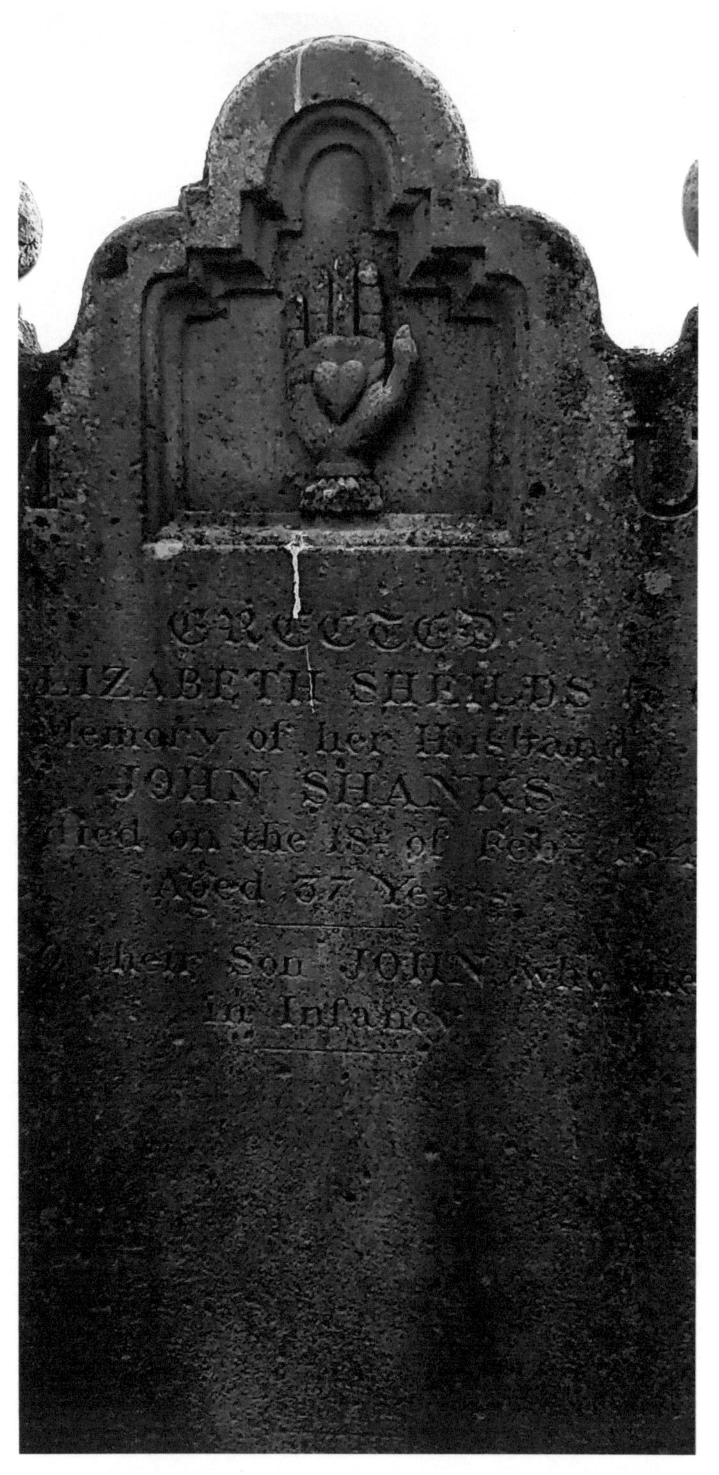

ERECTED
ELIZABETH SHIELDS
Memory of her Husband
JOHN SHANKS
died on the 1st of Feb
Aged 37 Years
their Son JOHN
in Infanc

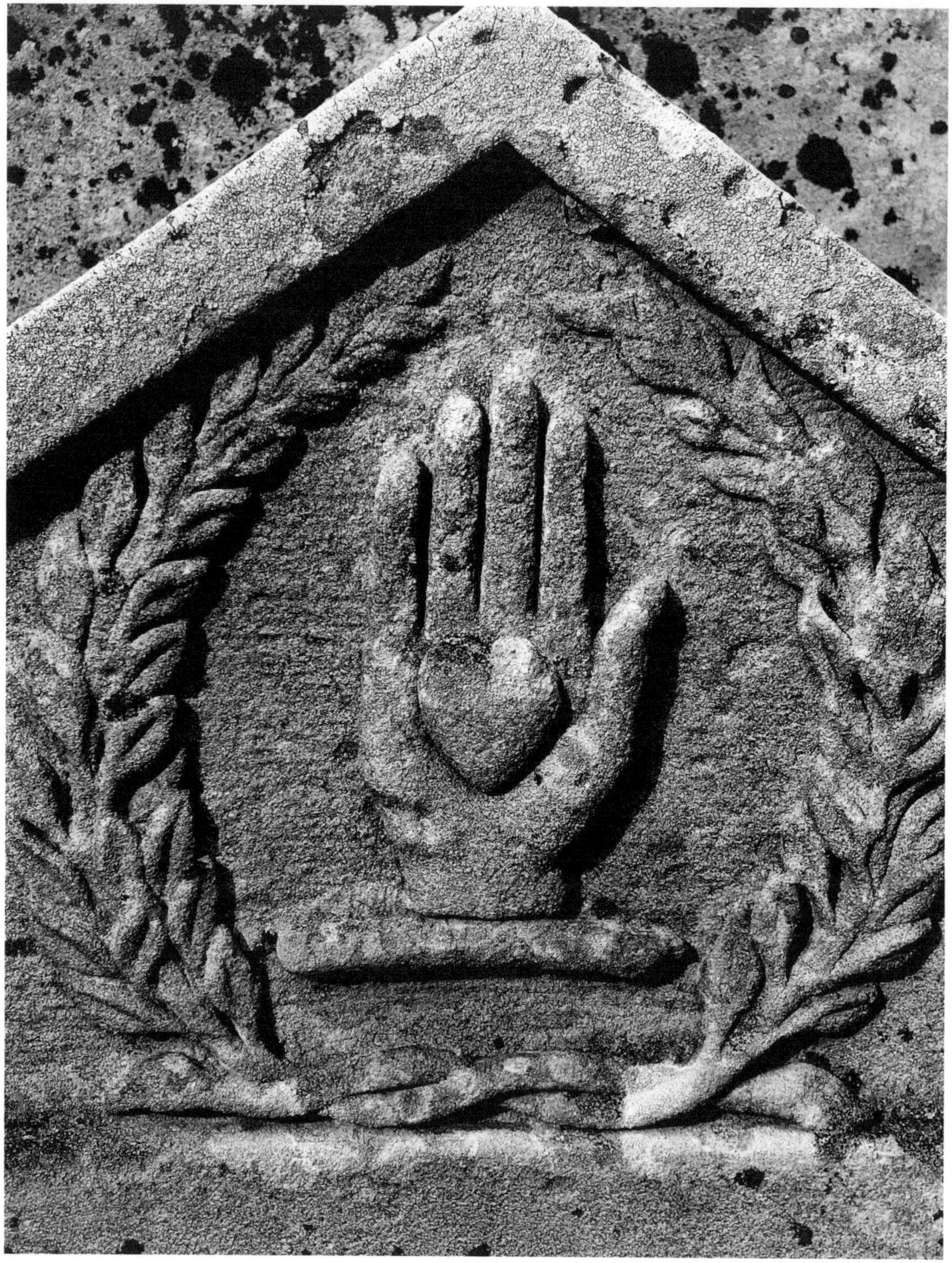

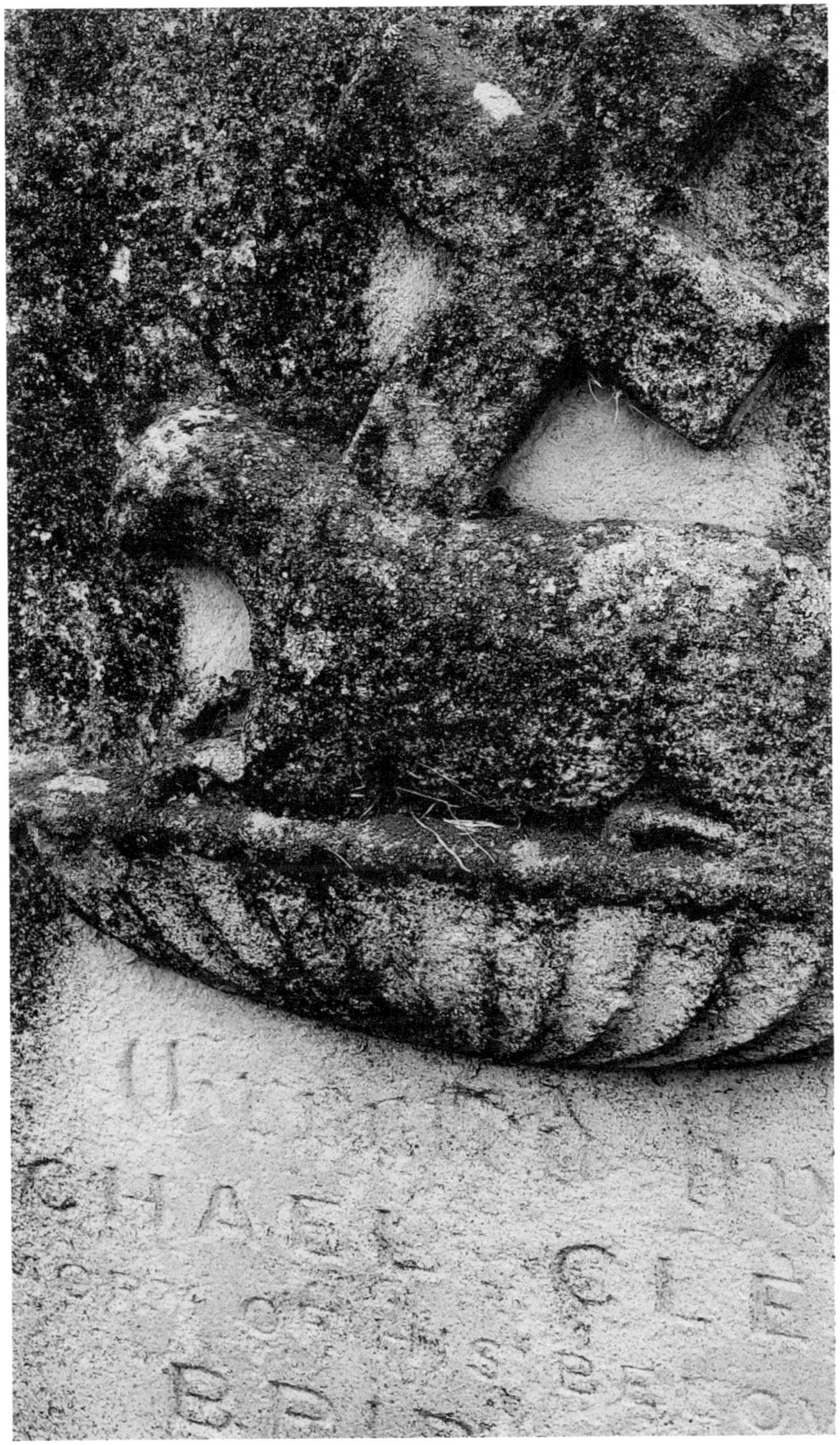

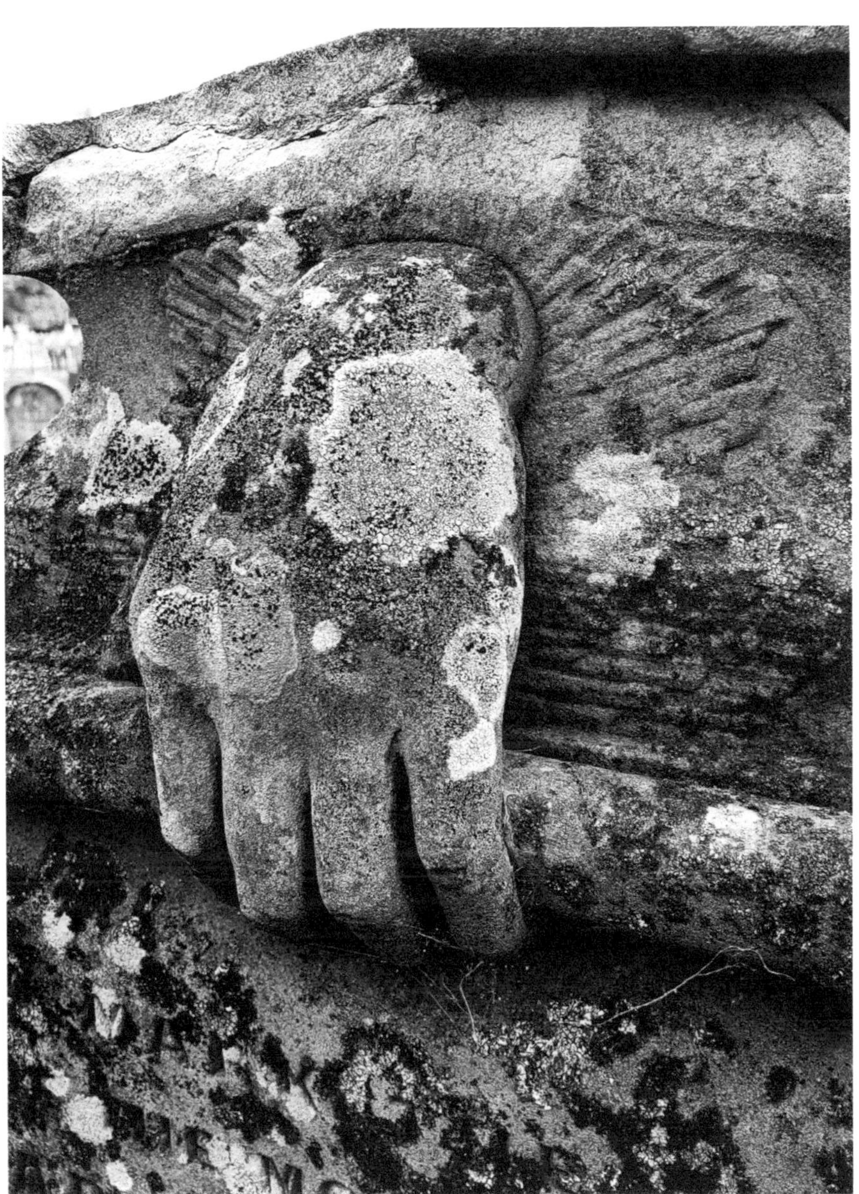

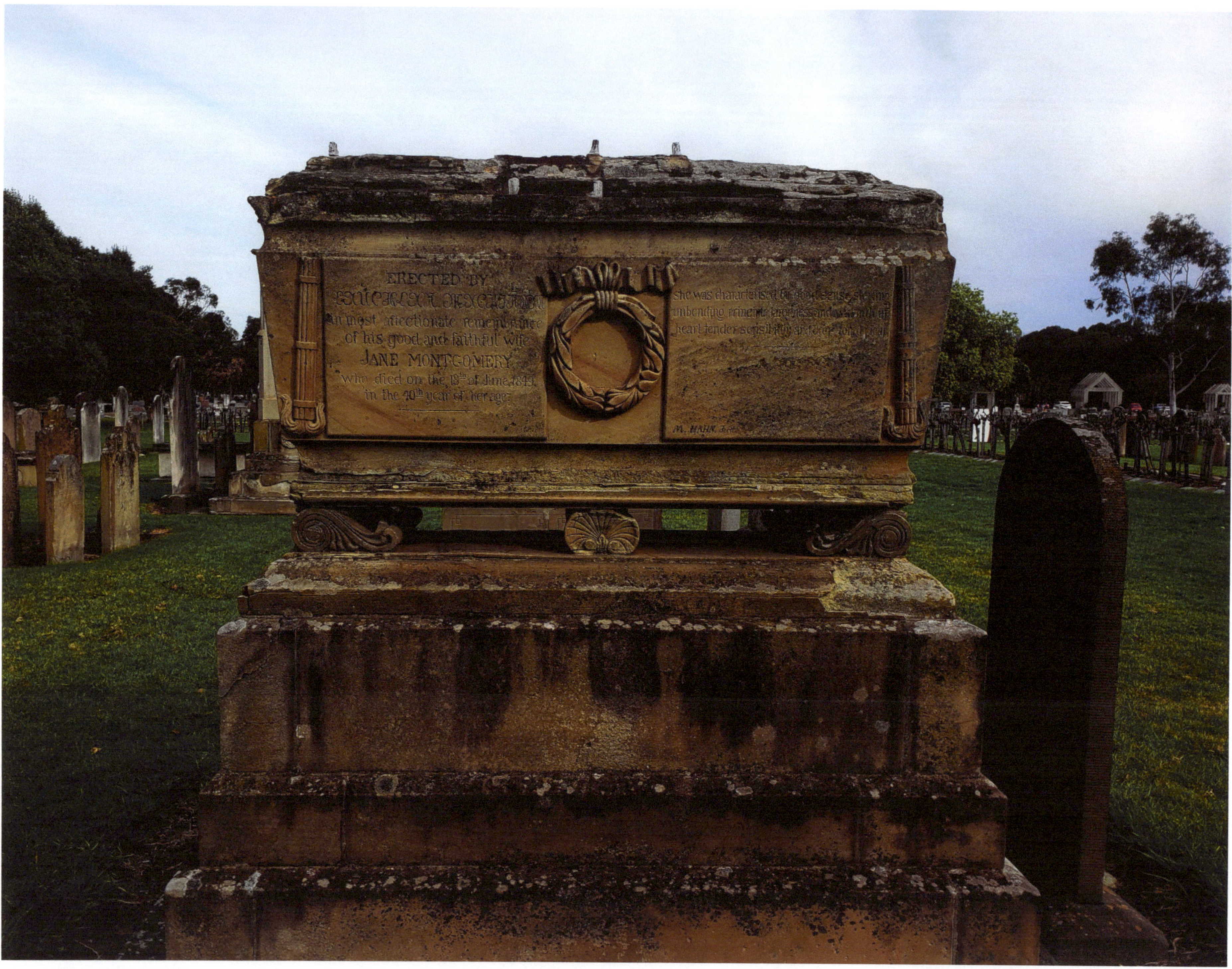

ERECTED BY
[...] an most affectionate remembrance
of his good and faithful wife
JANE MONTGOMERY
who died on the 18th of June 1849
in the 40th year of her age.
she was characterised
unbending principle
heart tender sensibility
M. HAHN Sc

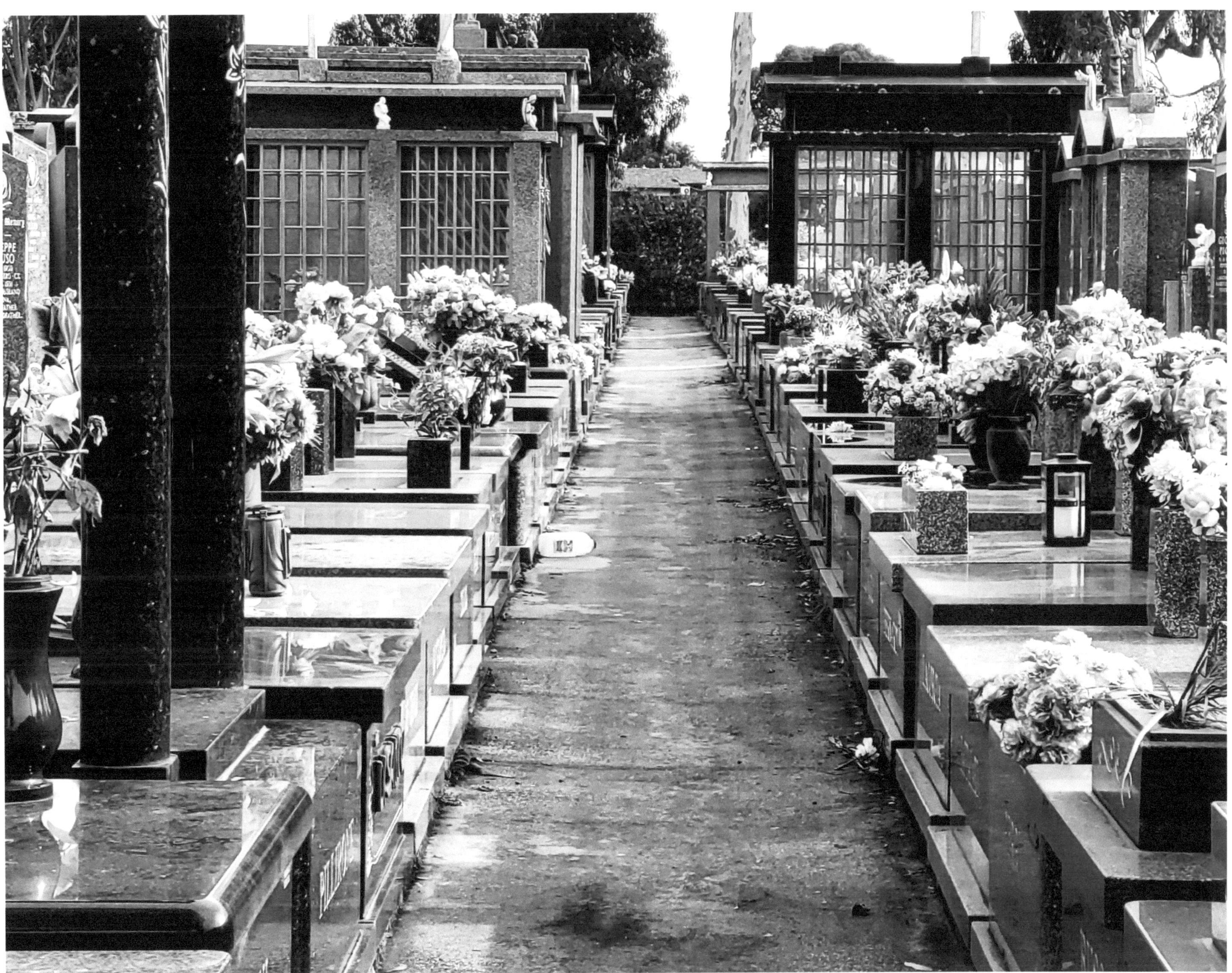

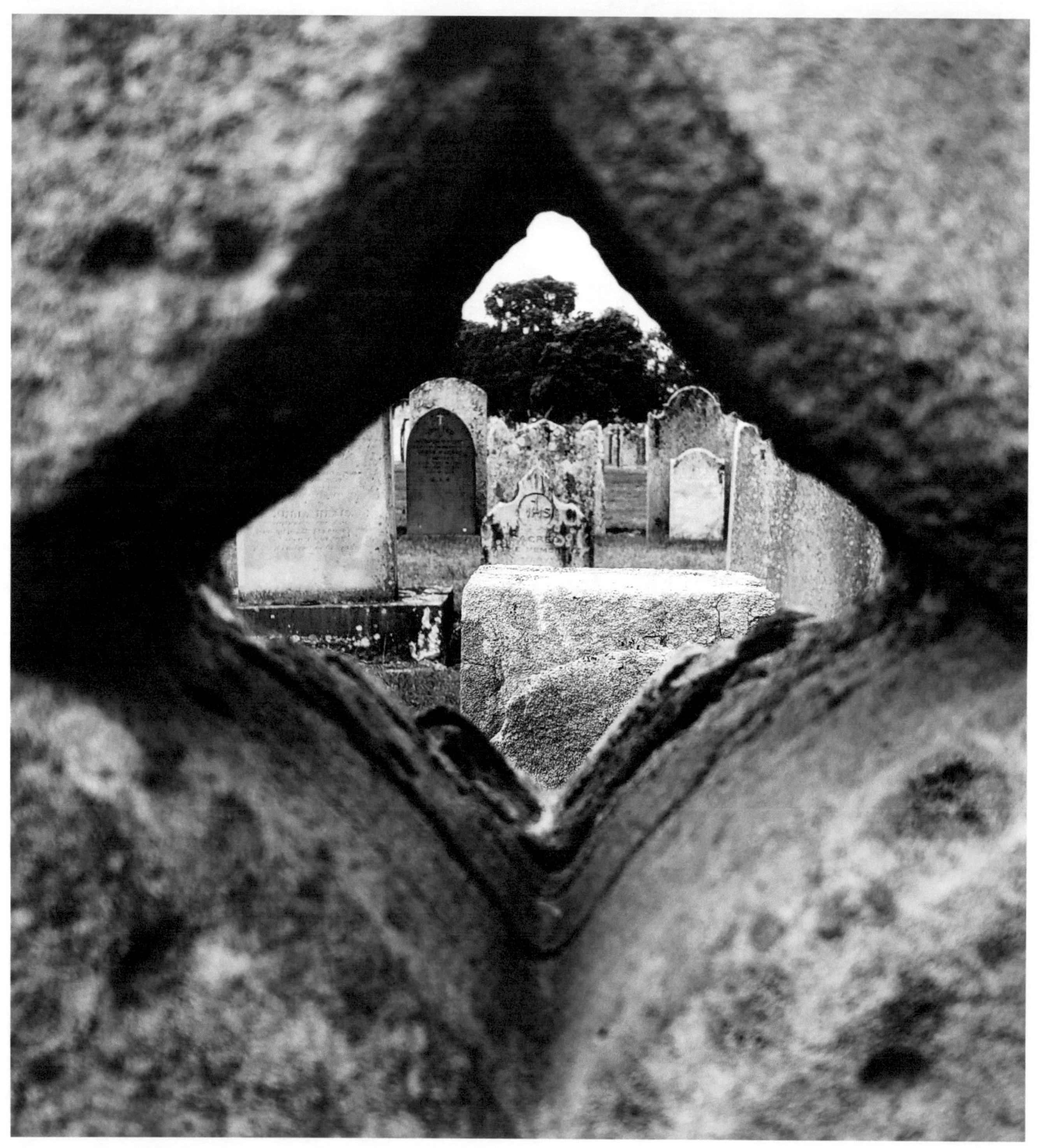

Footscray General Cemetery

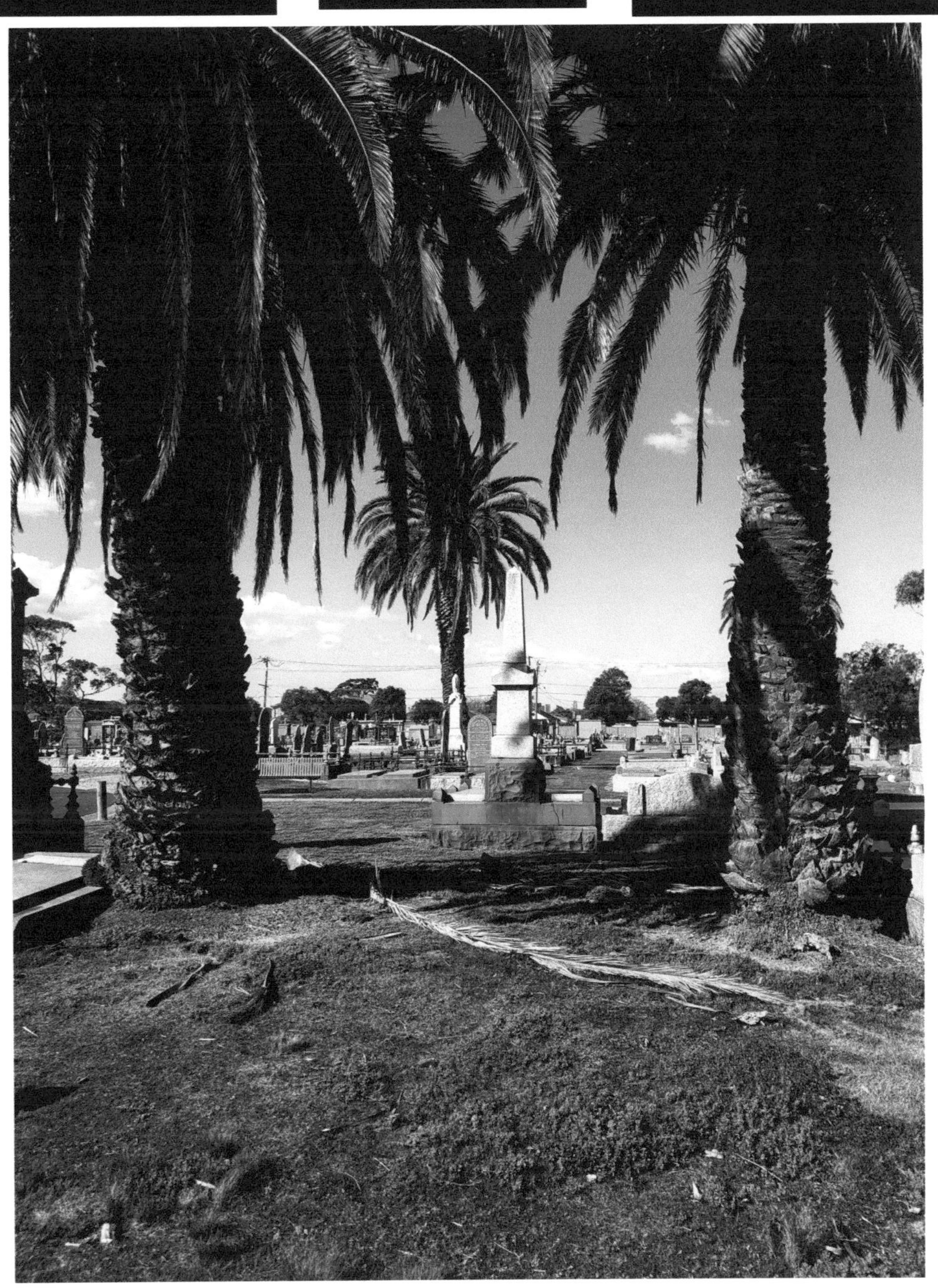

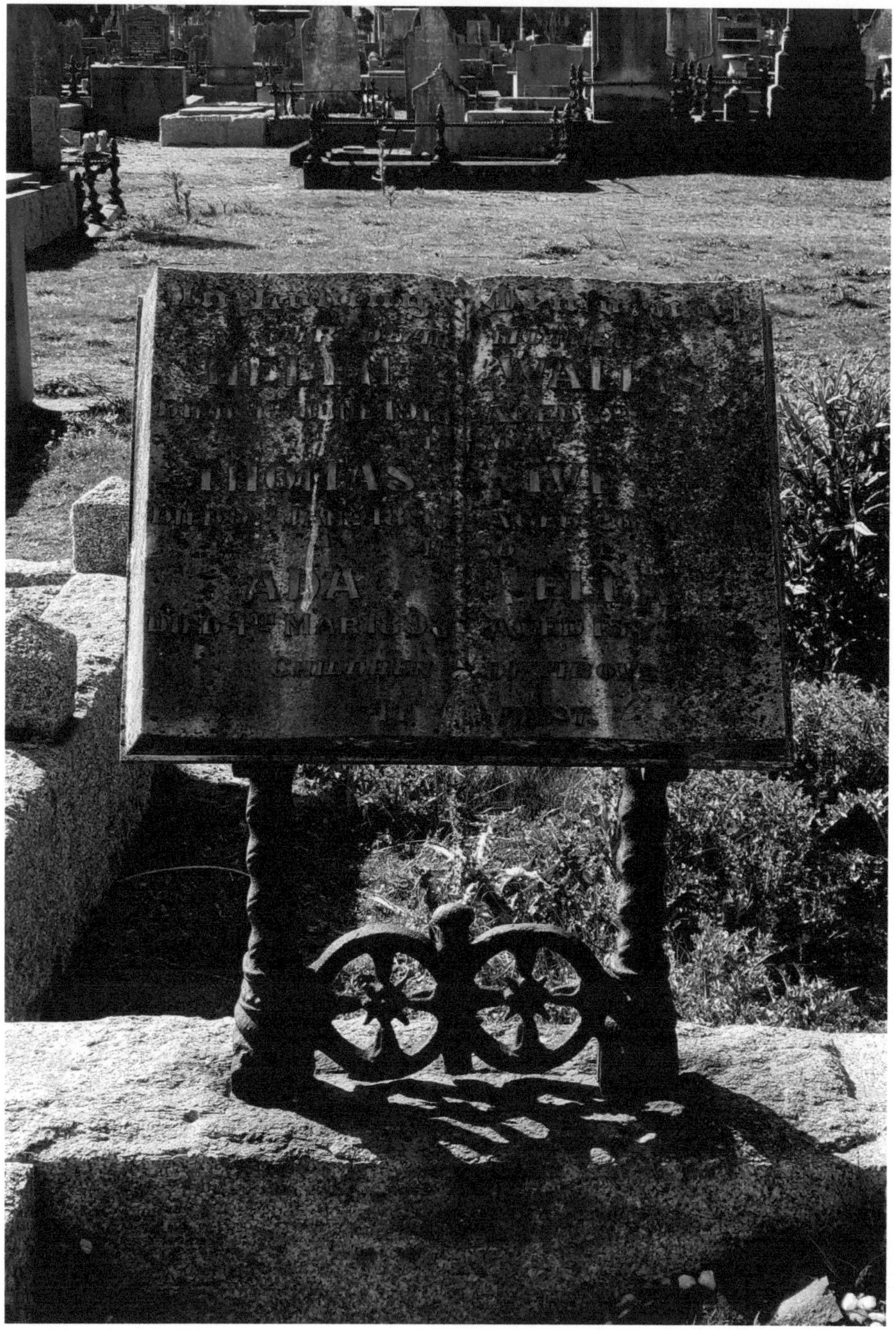

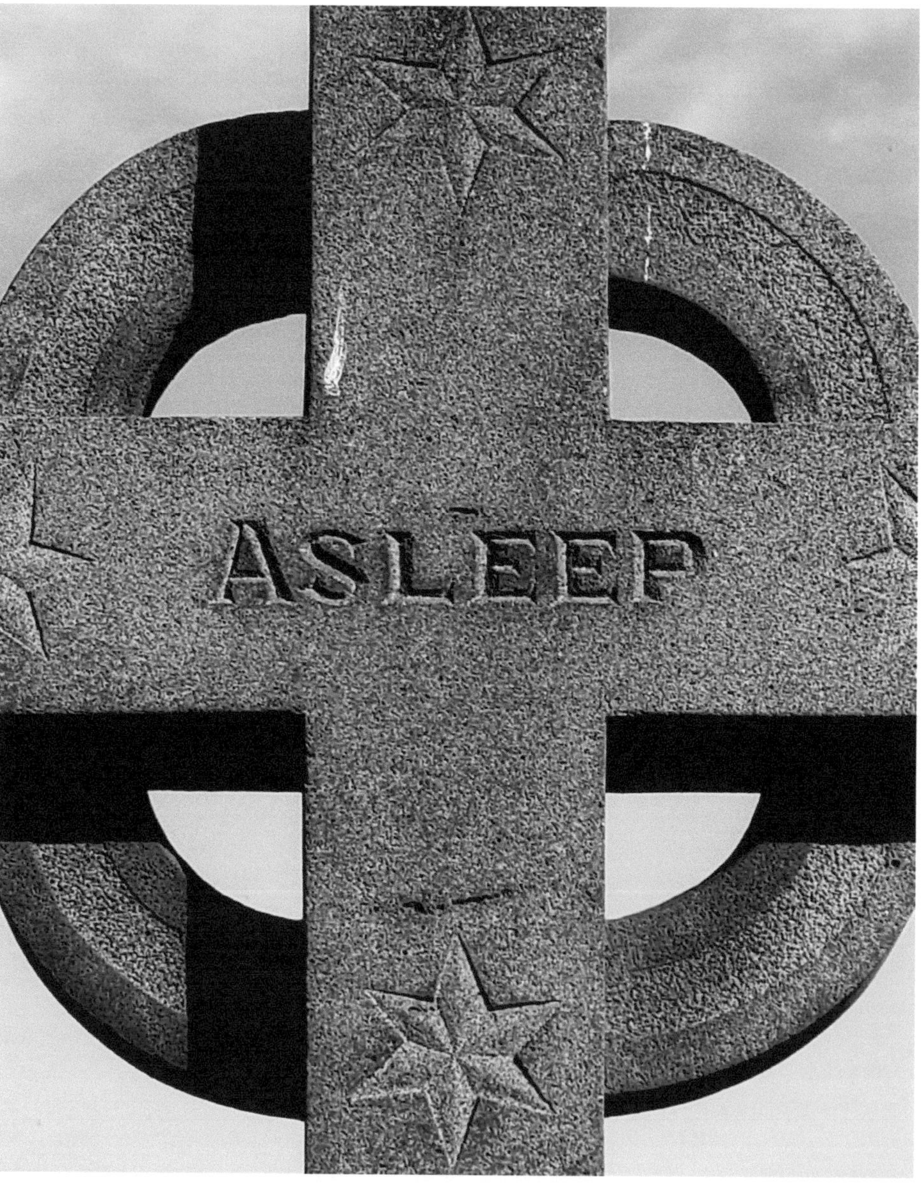

ASLEEP

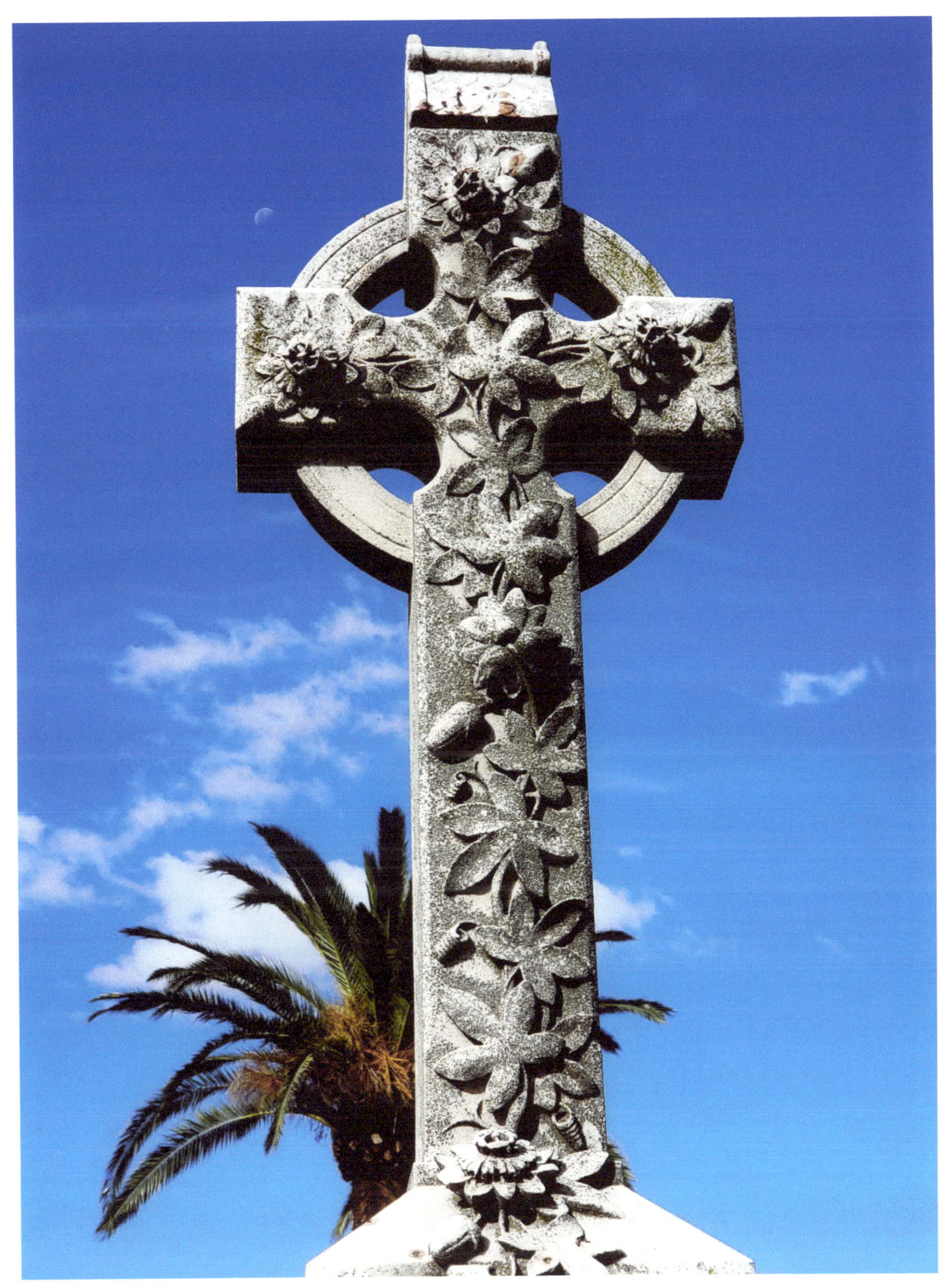

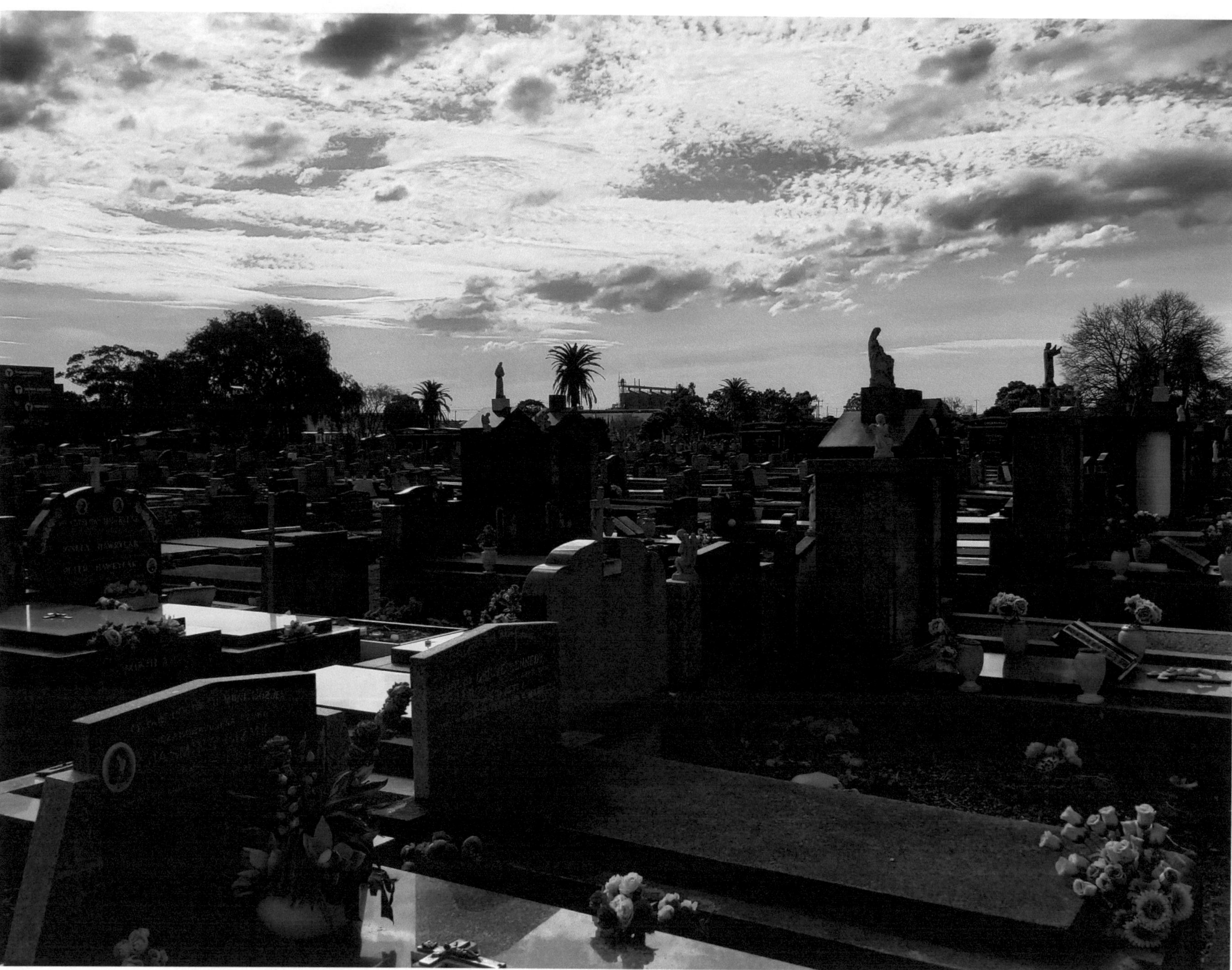

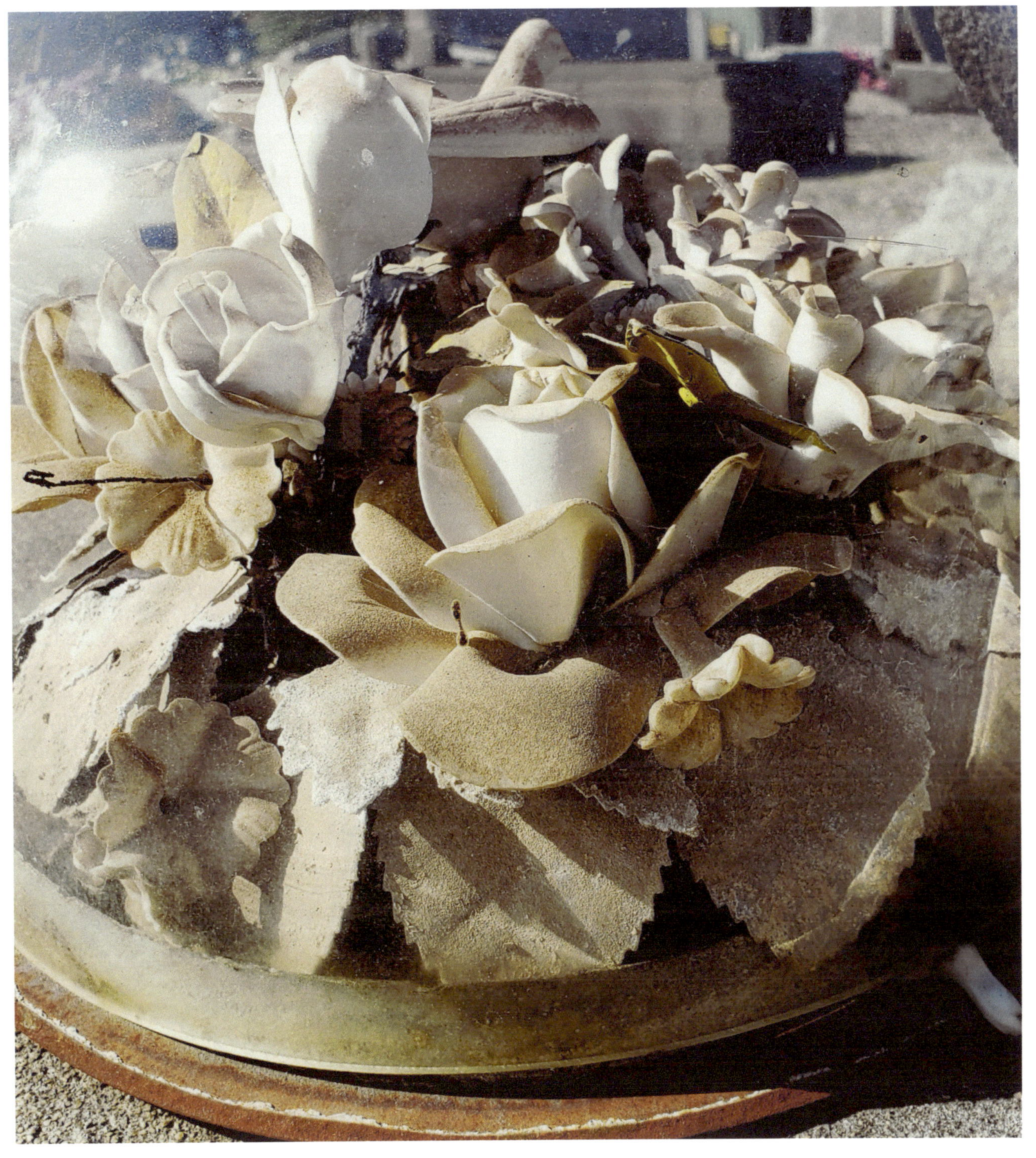

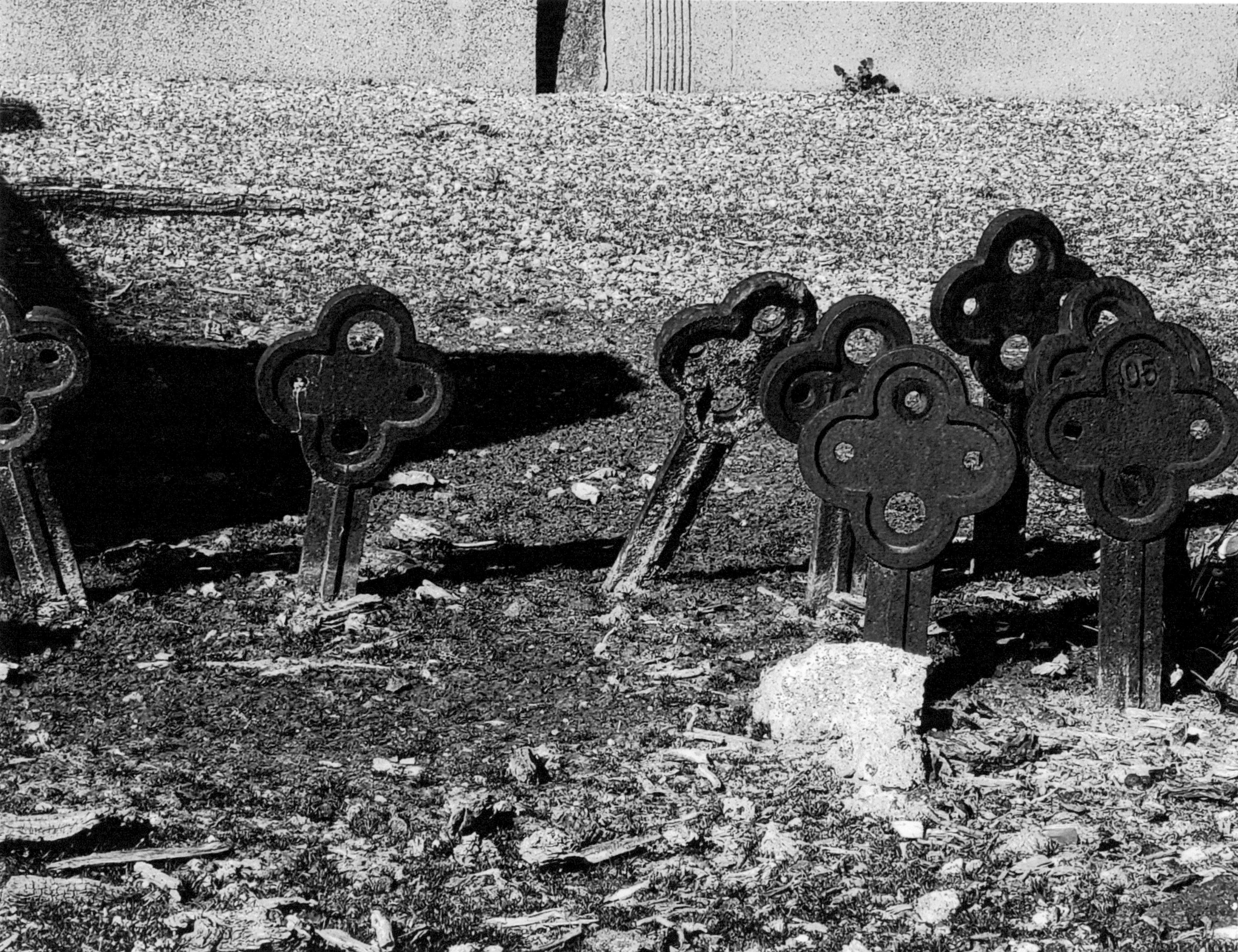

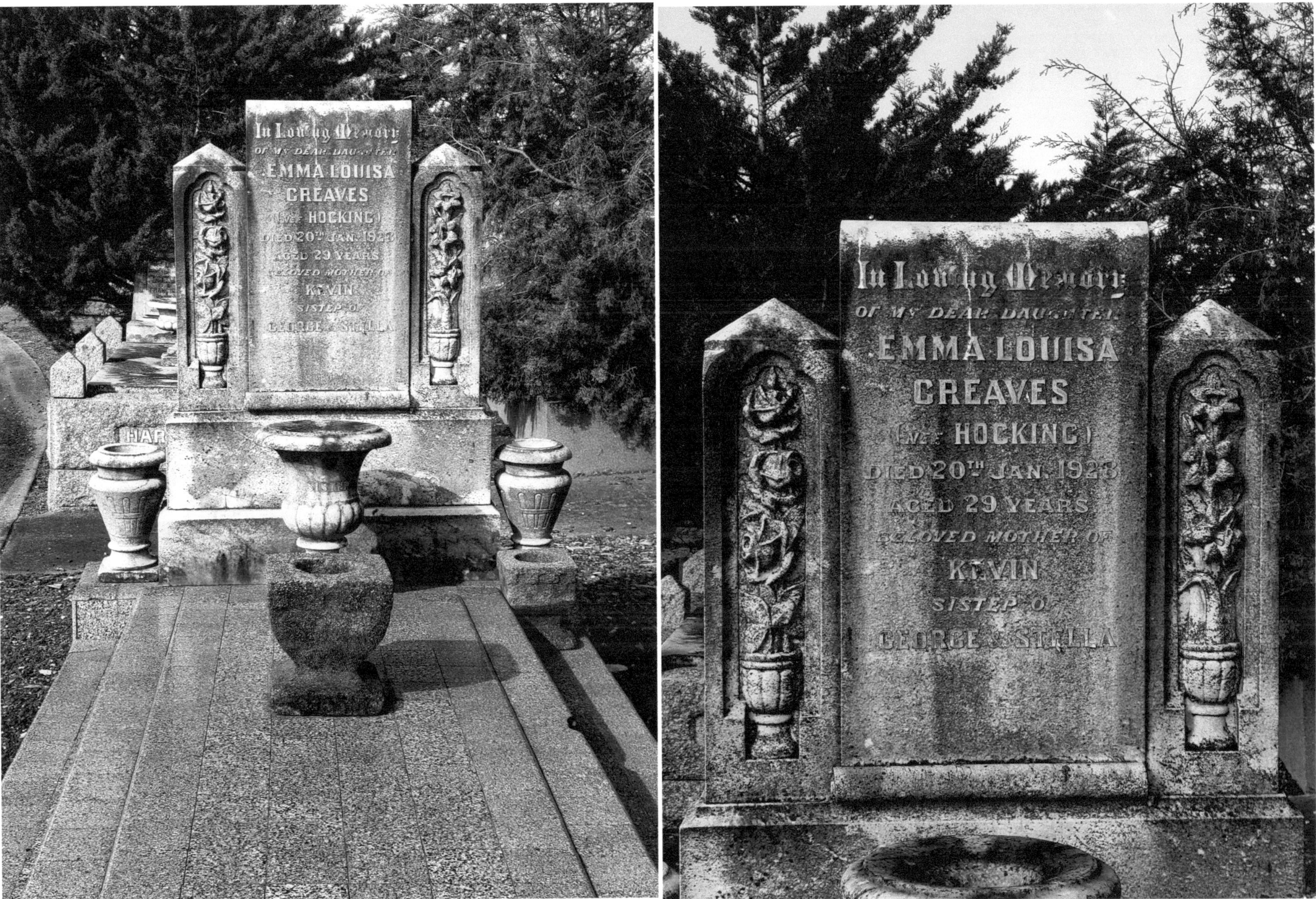
In Loving Memory
OF MY DEAR DAUGHTER
EMMA LOUISA
GREAVES
(NEE HOCKING)
DIED 20TH JAN. 1923
AGED 29 YEARS
BELOVED MOTHER OF
KEVIN
SISTER O
GEORGE & STELLA

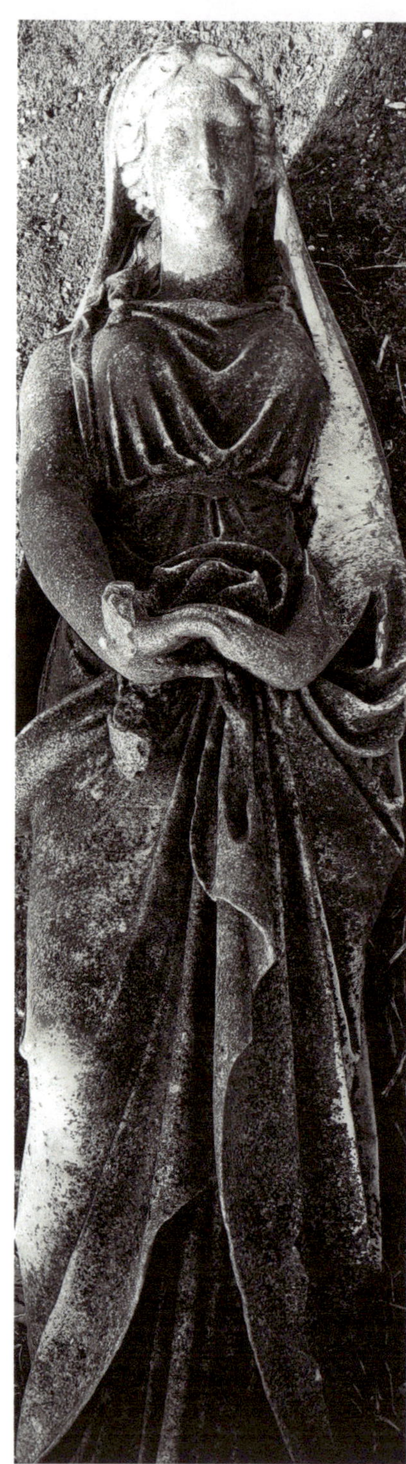

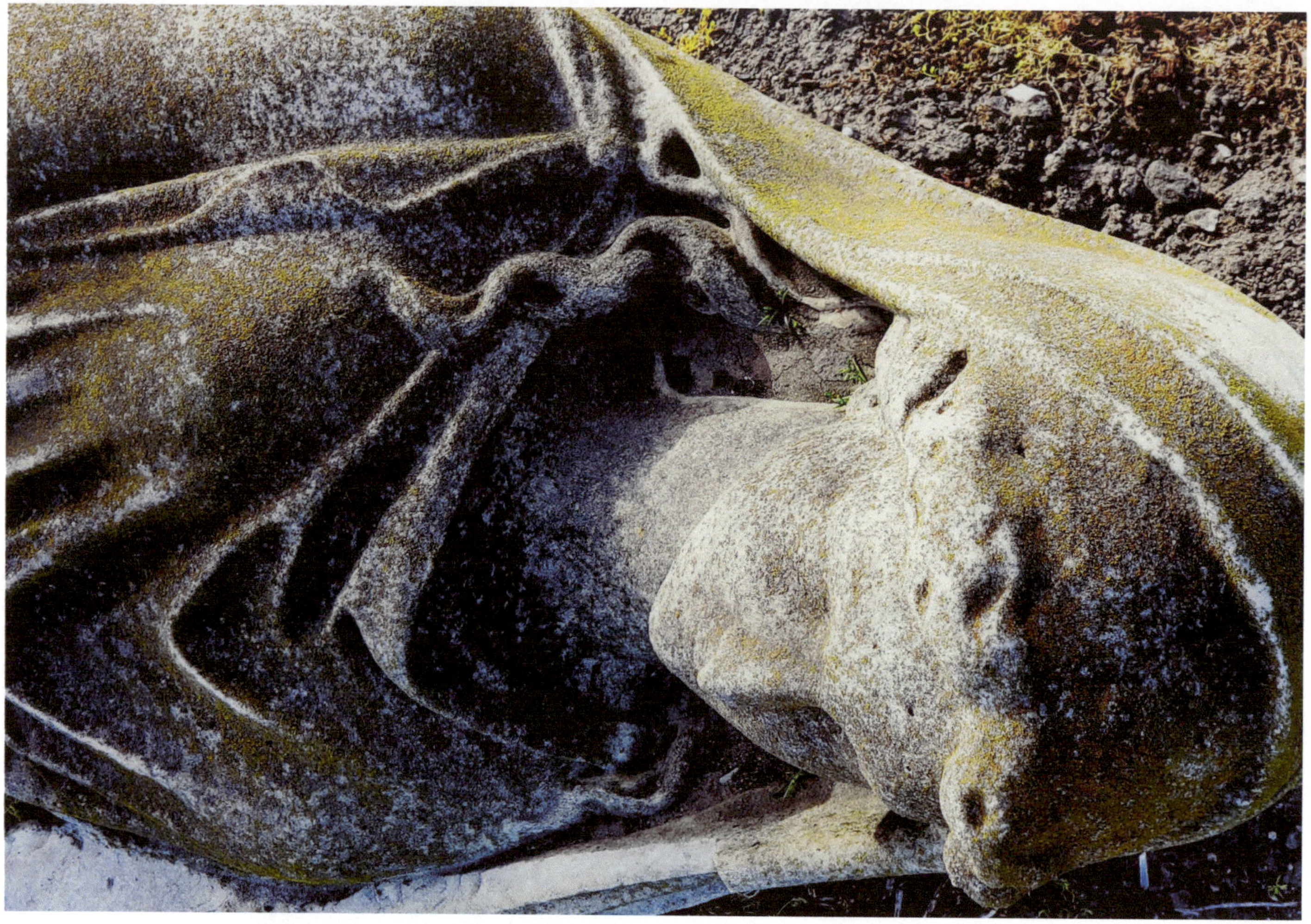

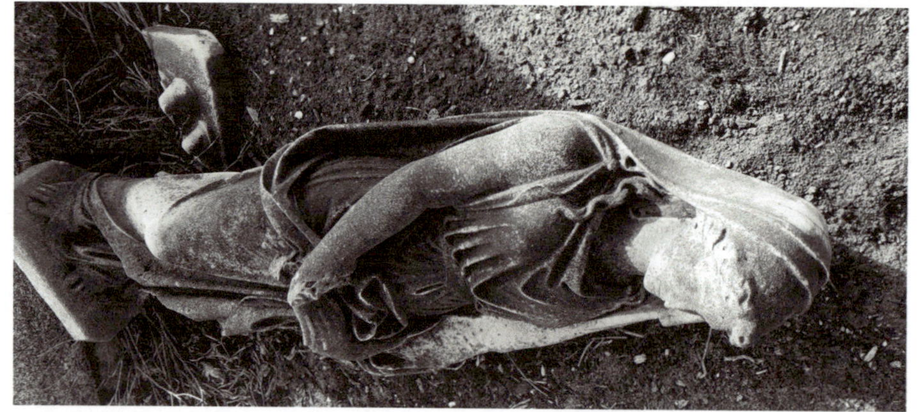

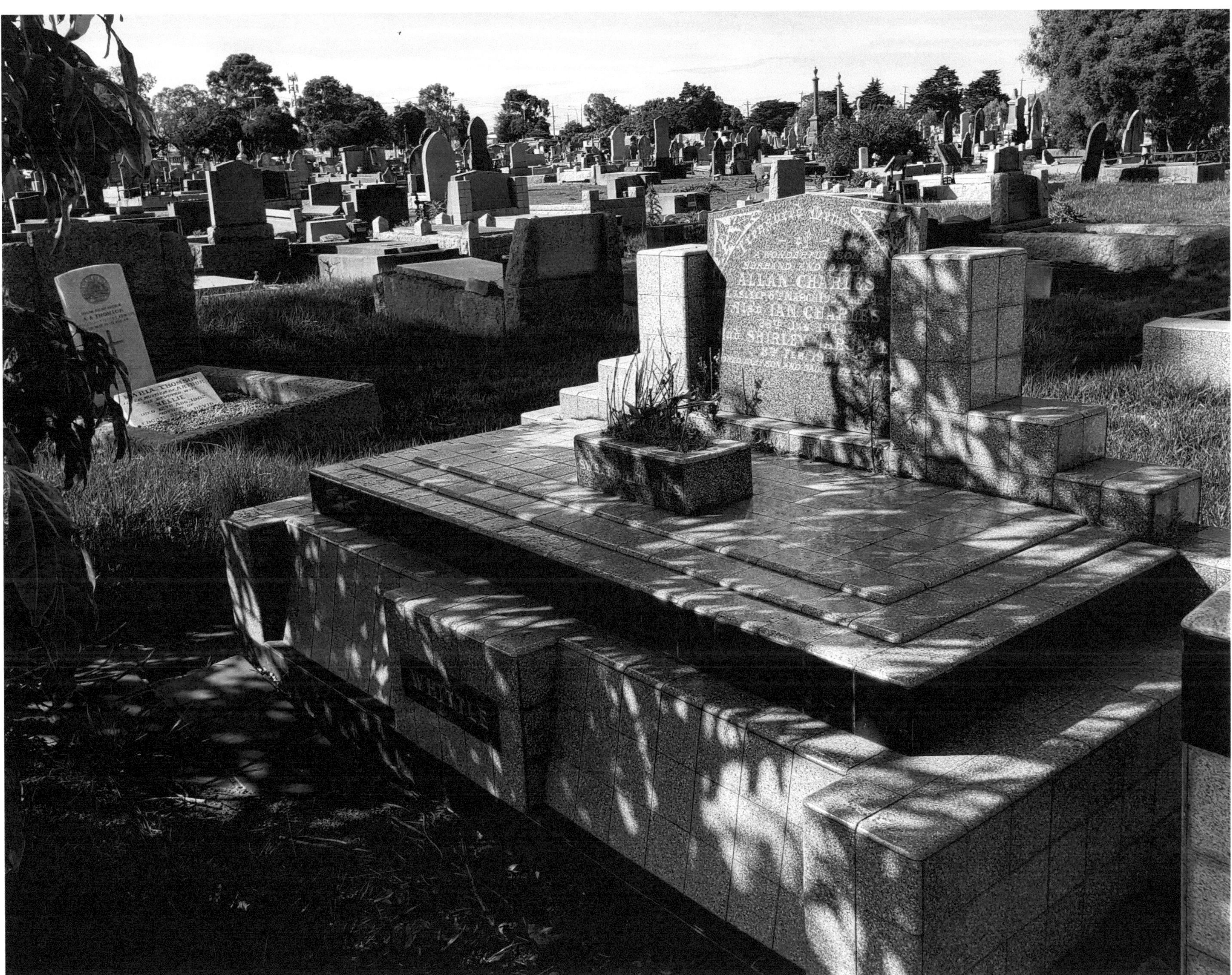

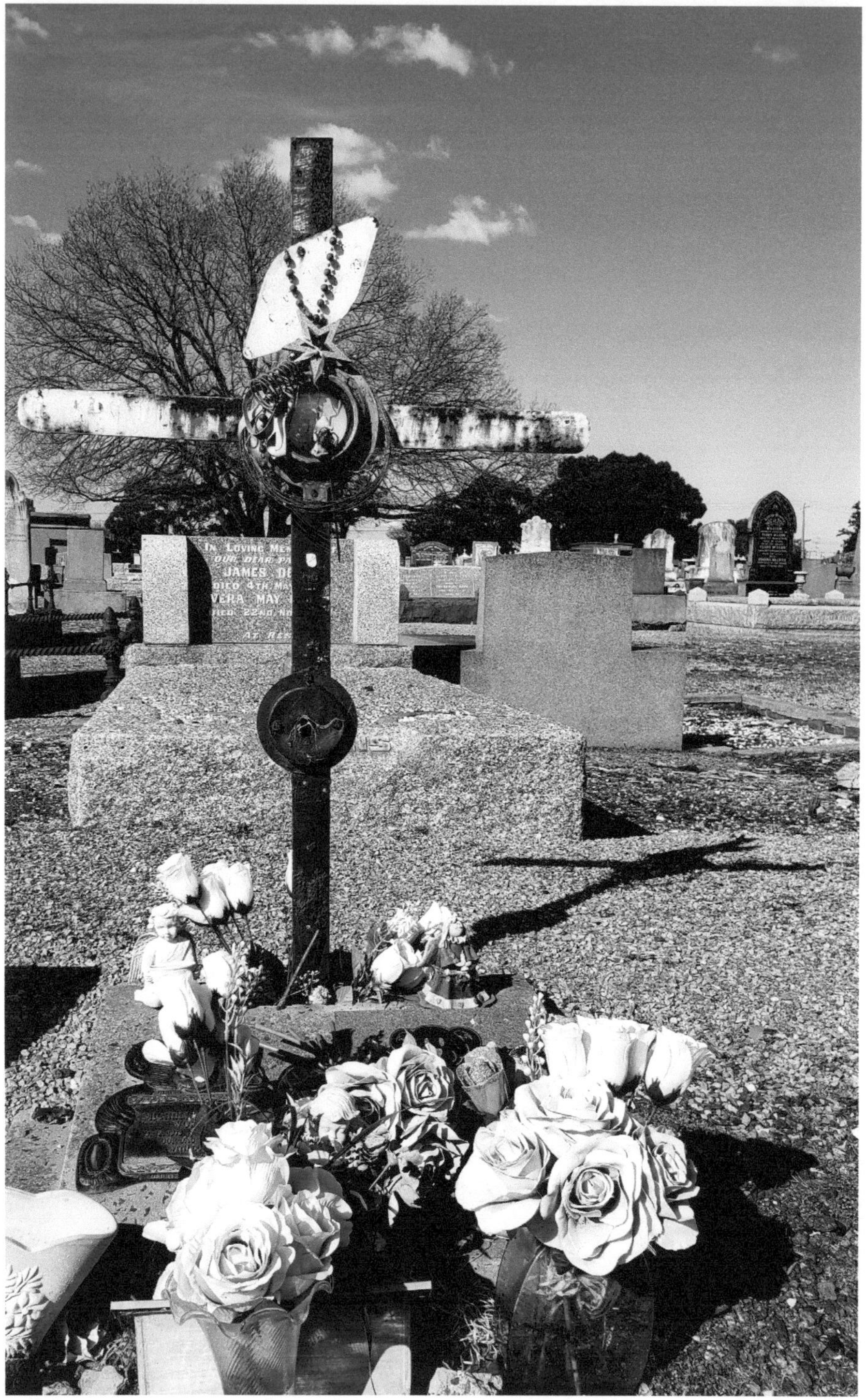

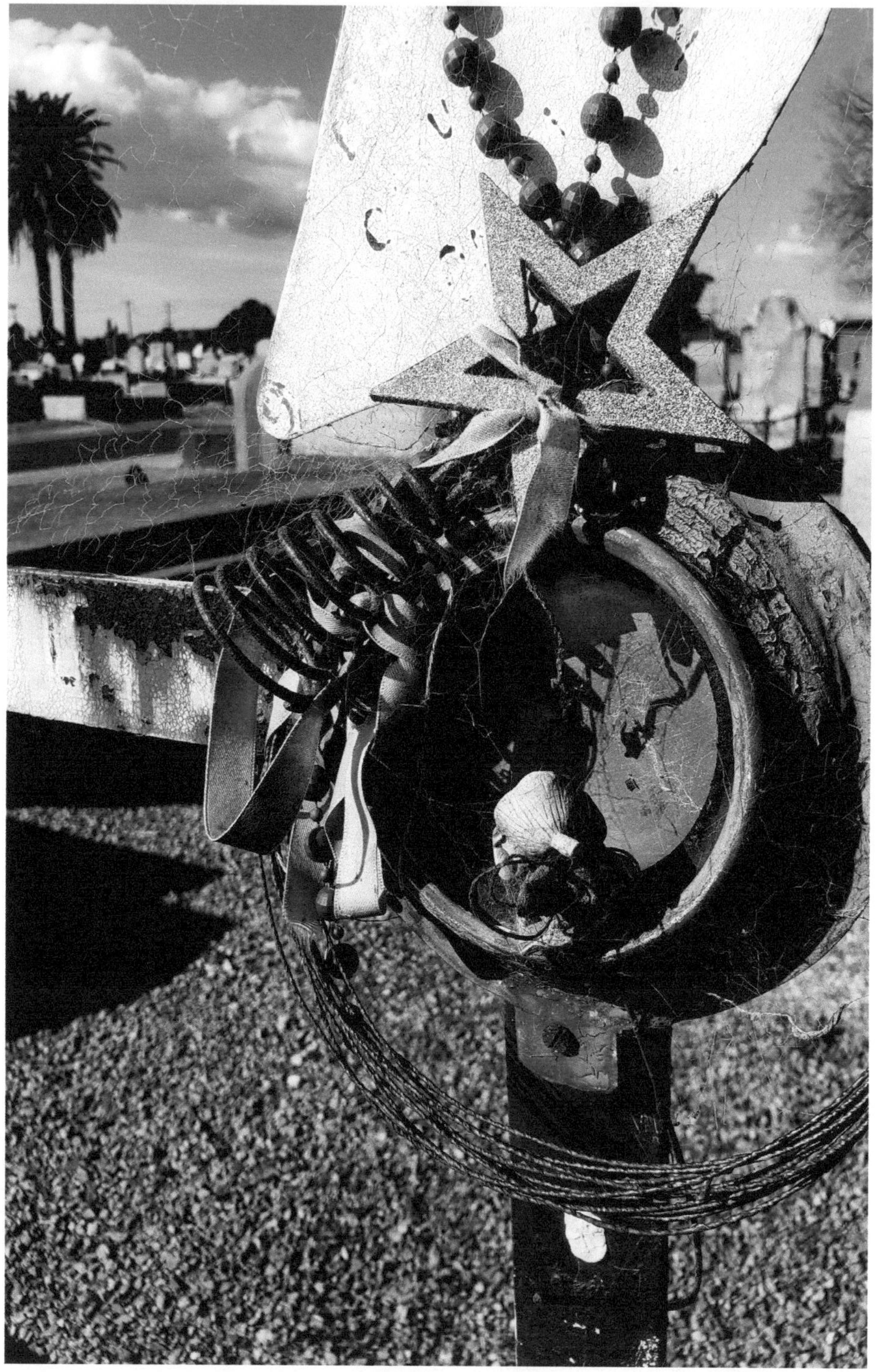

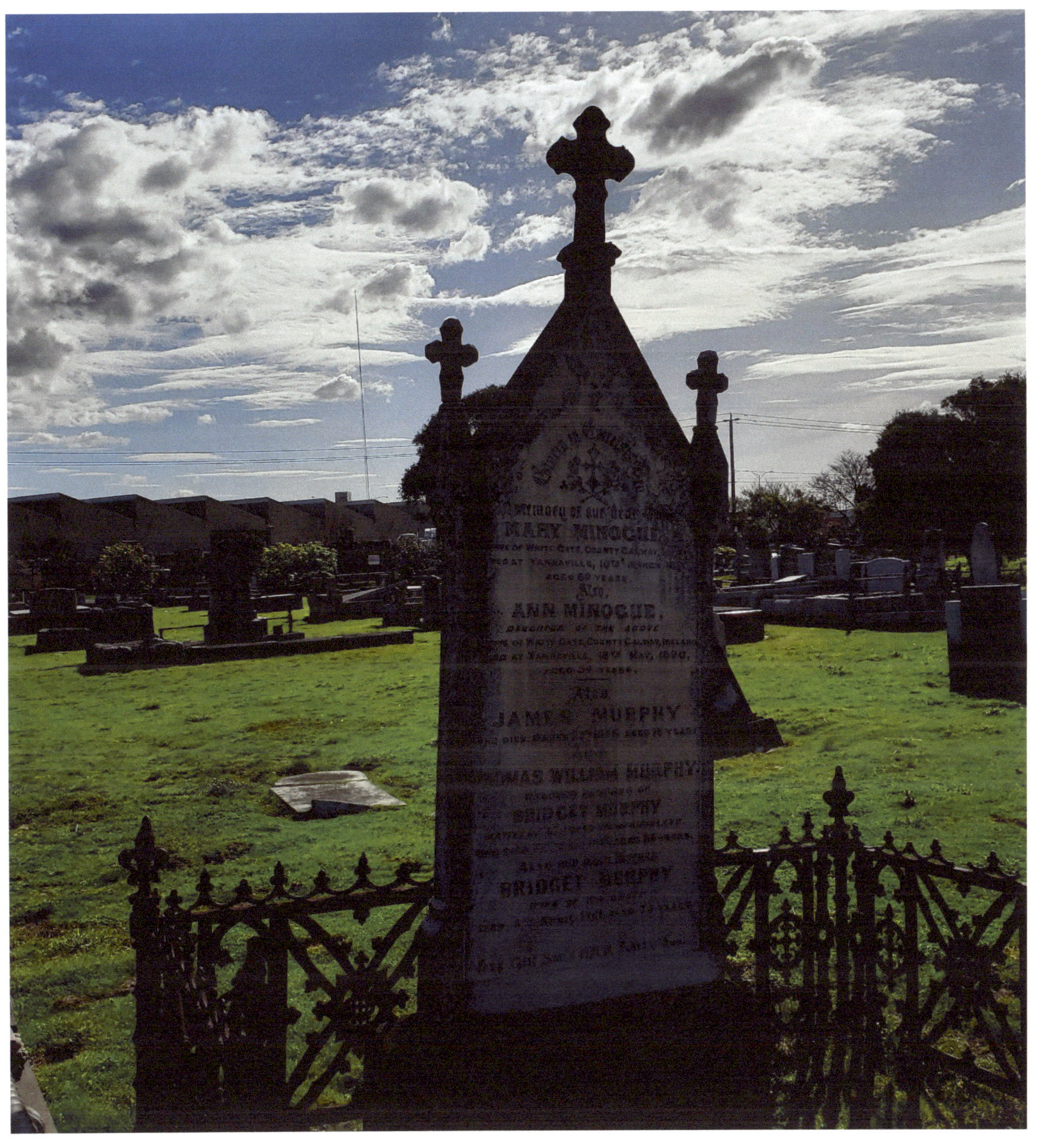
In memory of our dear mother
MARY MINOGUE
native of White Gate, County Galway,
died at Yarraville, 10th March
aged 68 years.
Also
ANN MINOGUE,
daughter of the above
native of White Gate, County Galway, Ireland
died at Yarraville, 18th May, 1890,
aged 34 years.
Also
JAMES MURPHY
who died
aged 18 years.
THOMAS WILLIAM MURPHY
BRIDGET MURPHY
BRIDGET MURPHY
aged 73 years

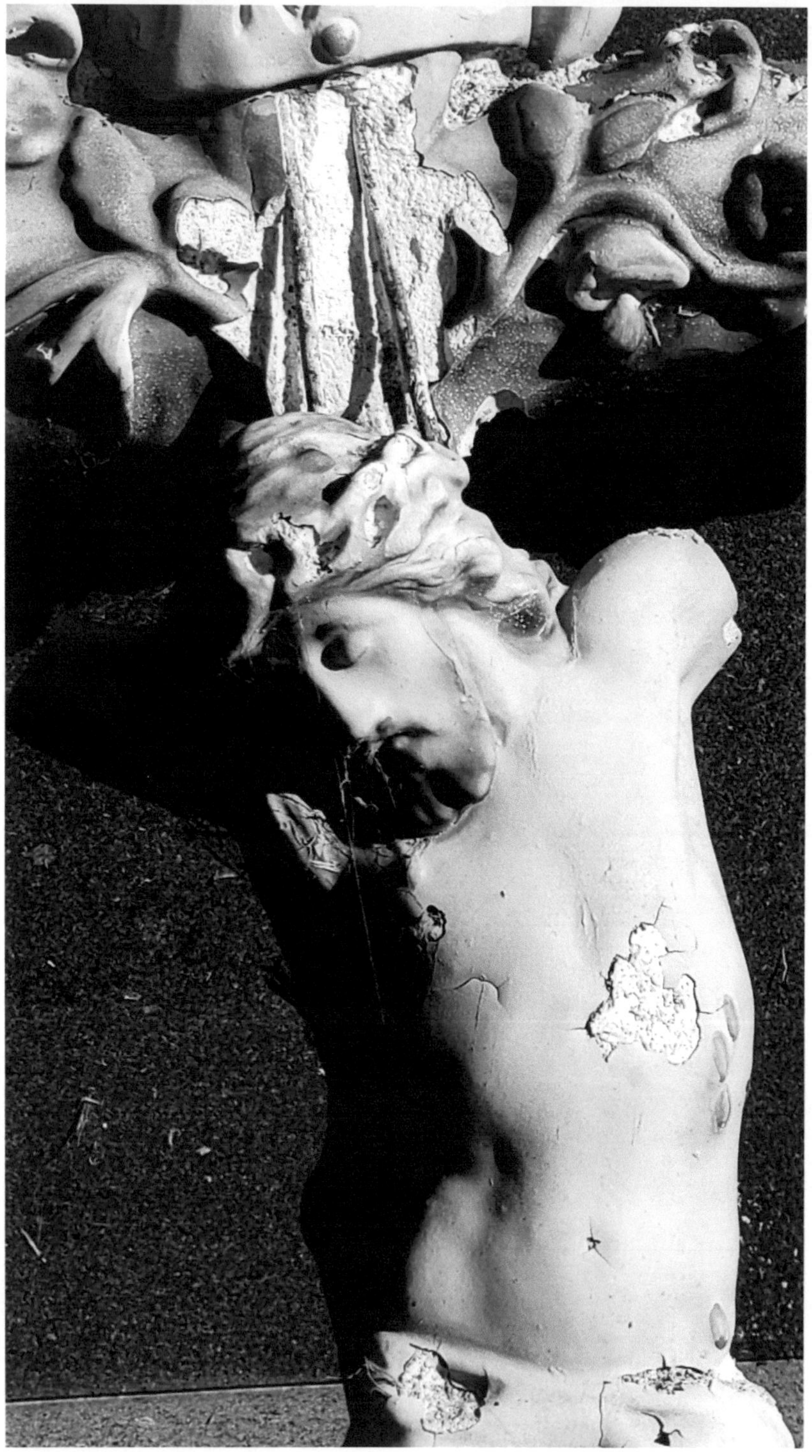

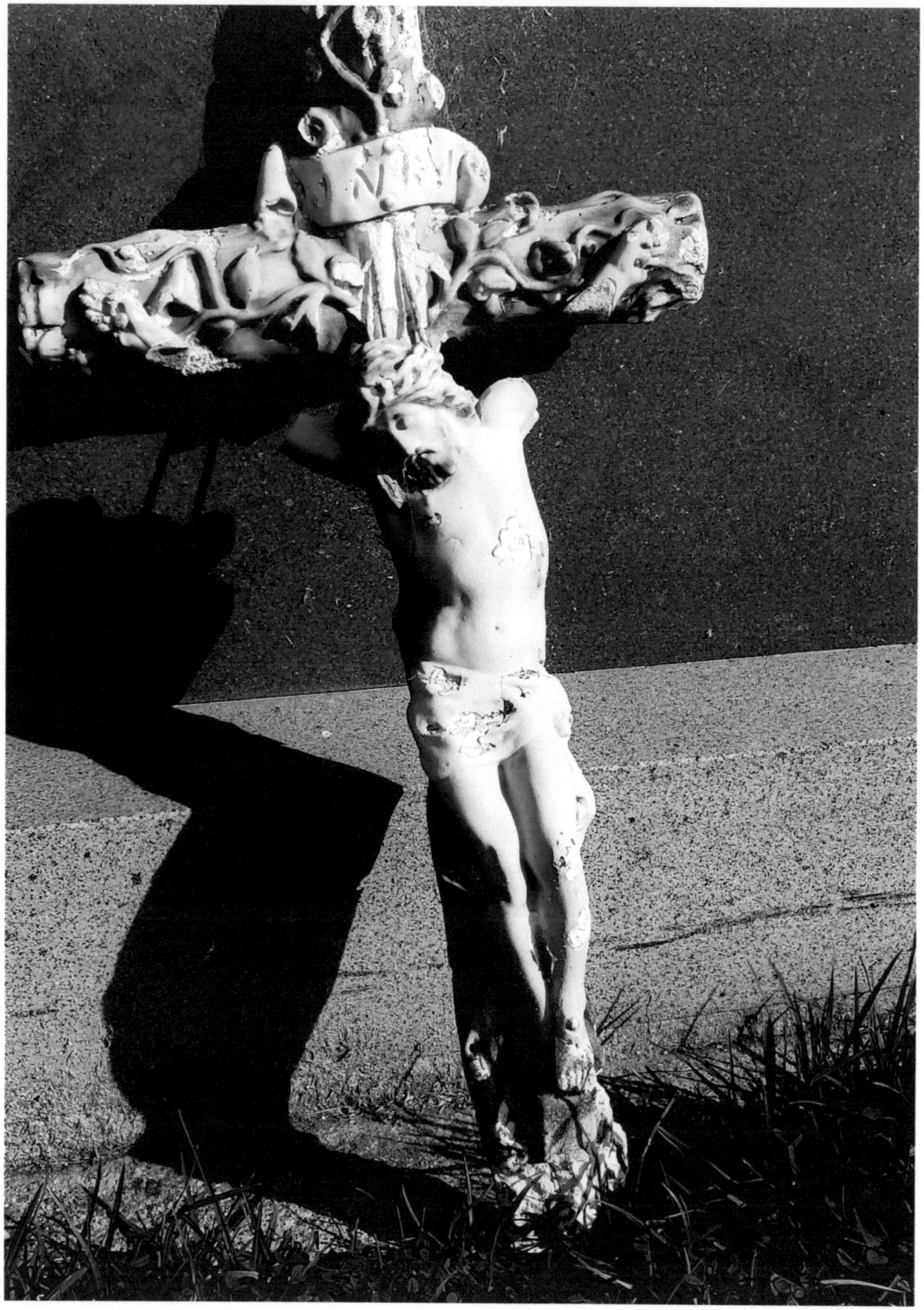

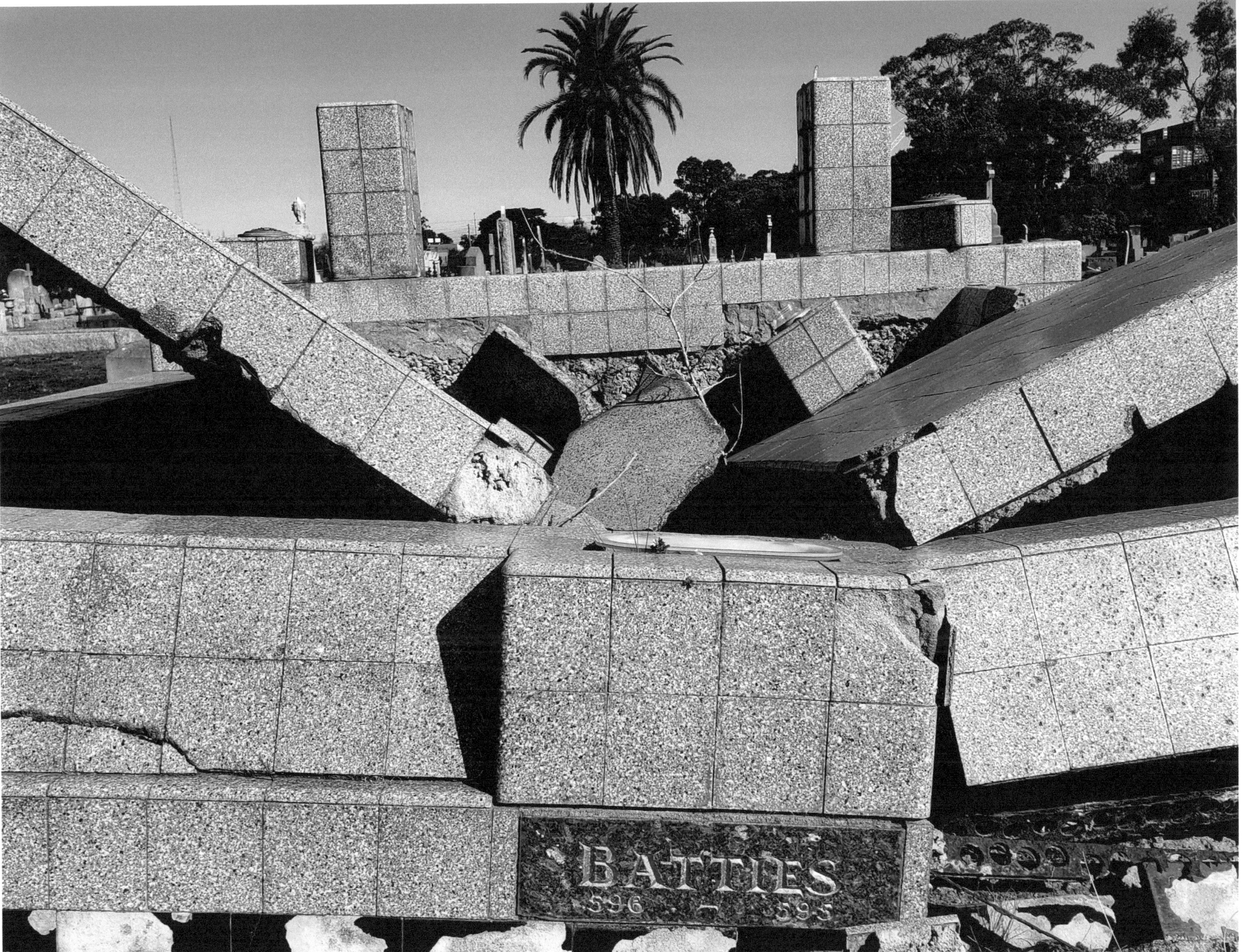
BATTIES
596 — 595

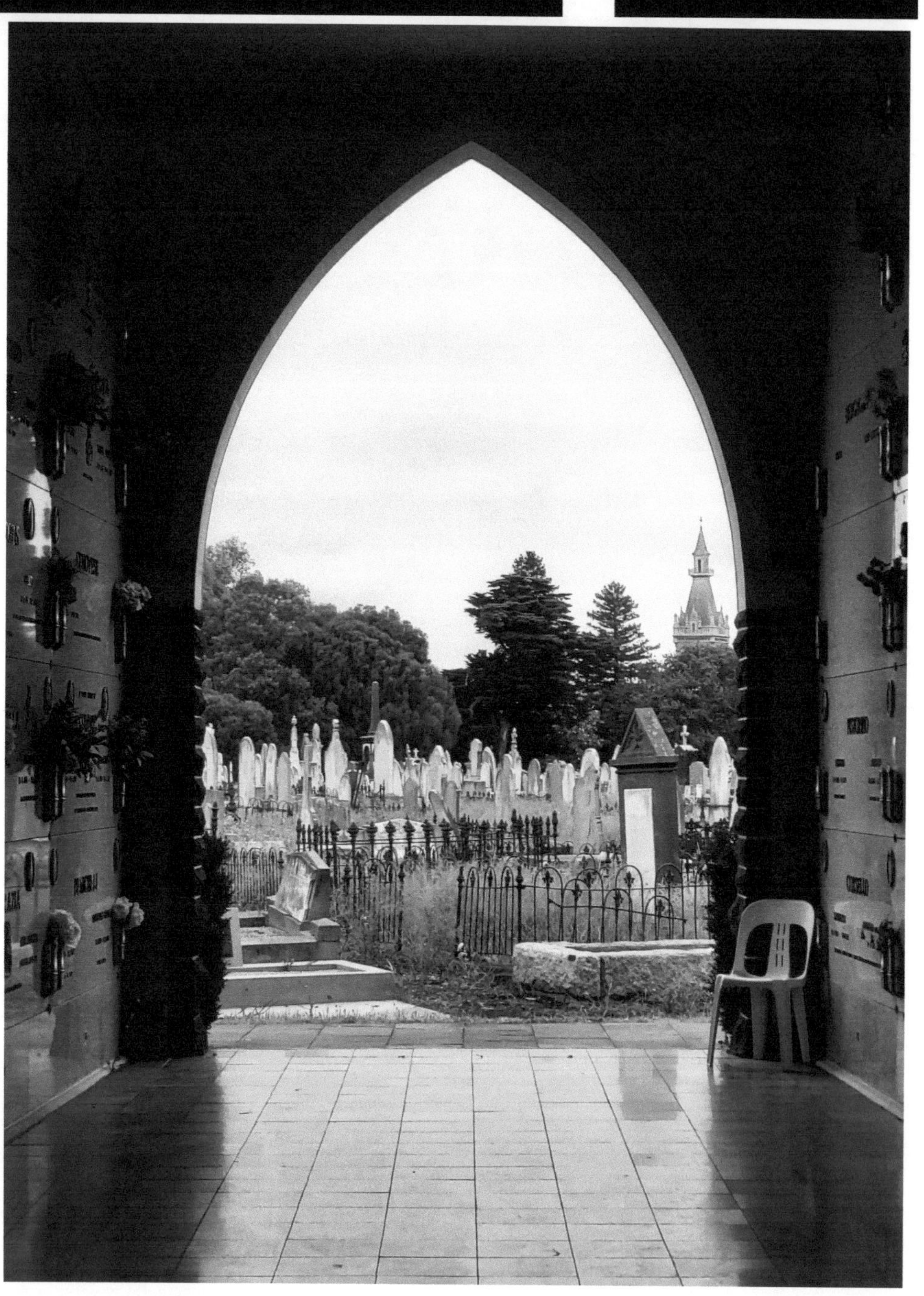

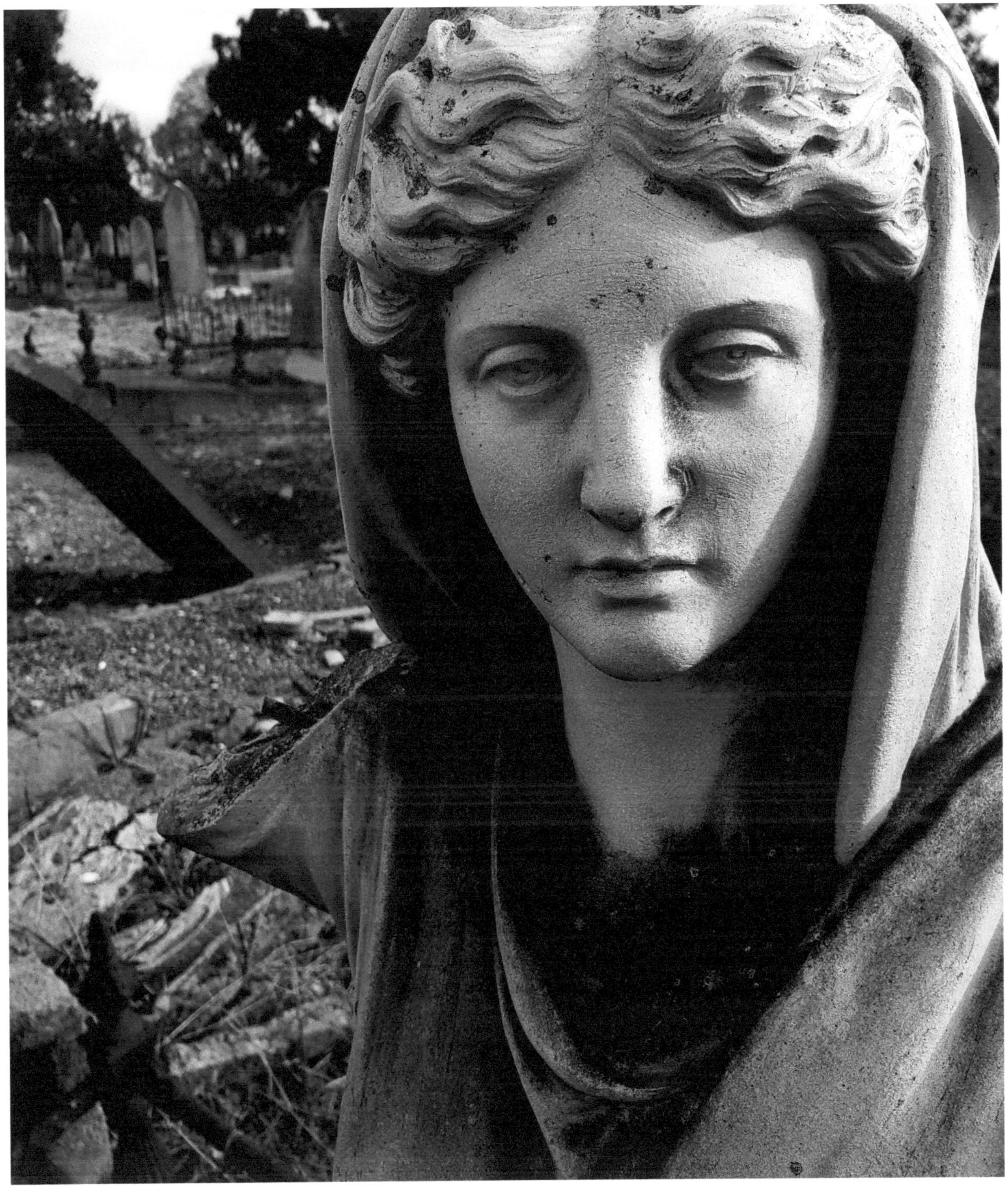

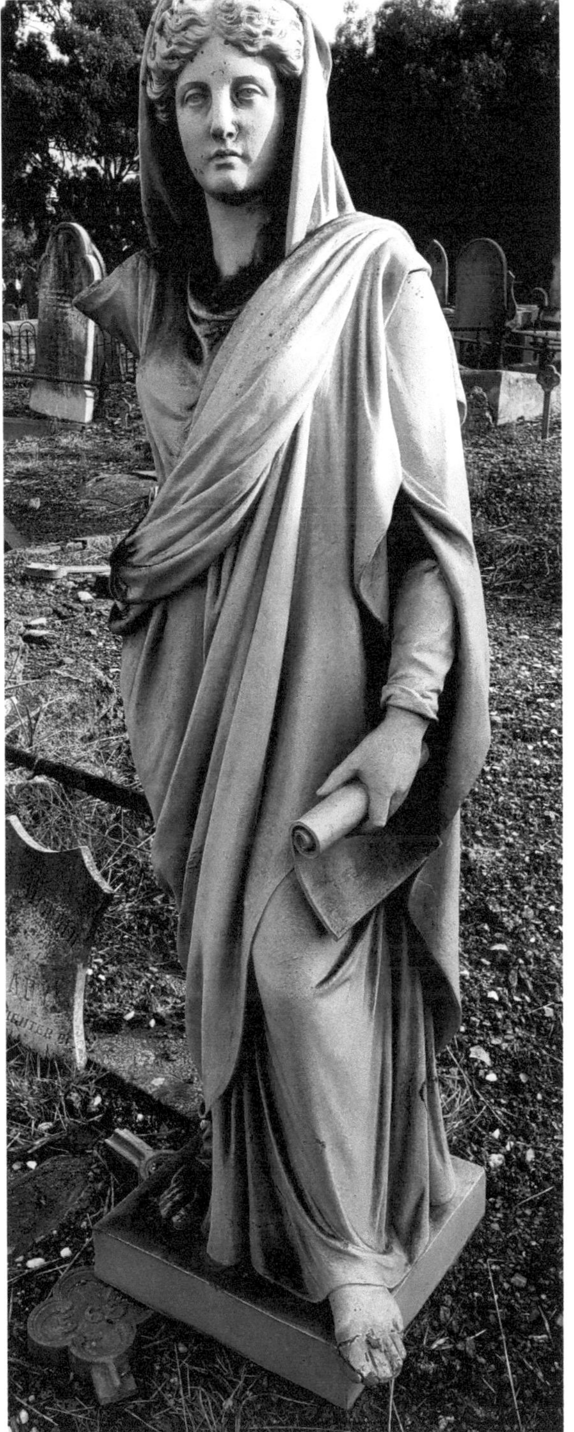

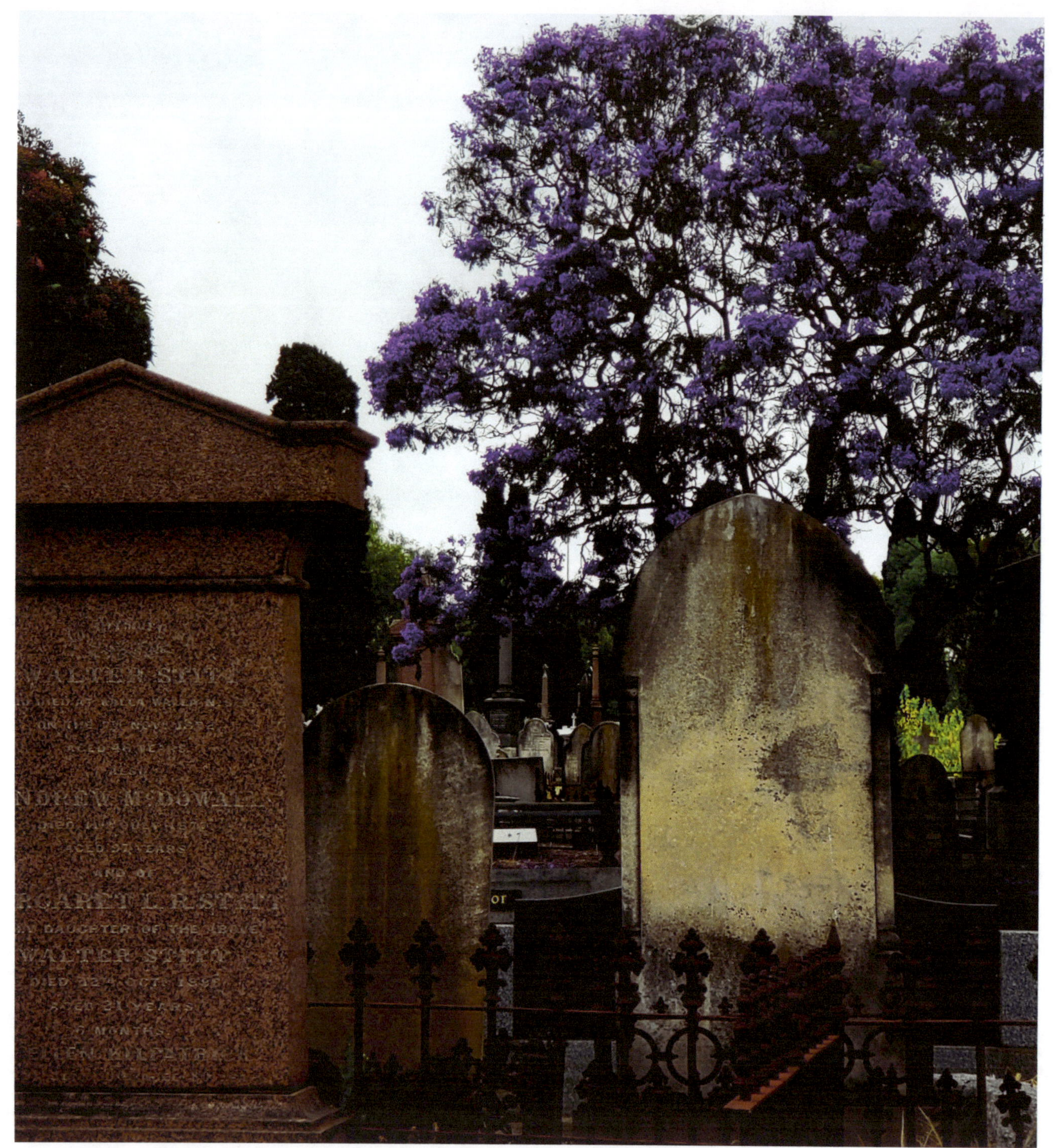

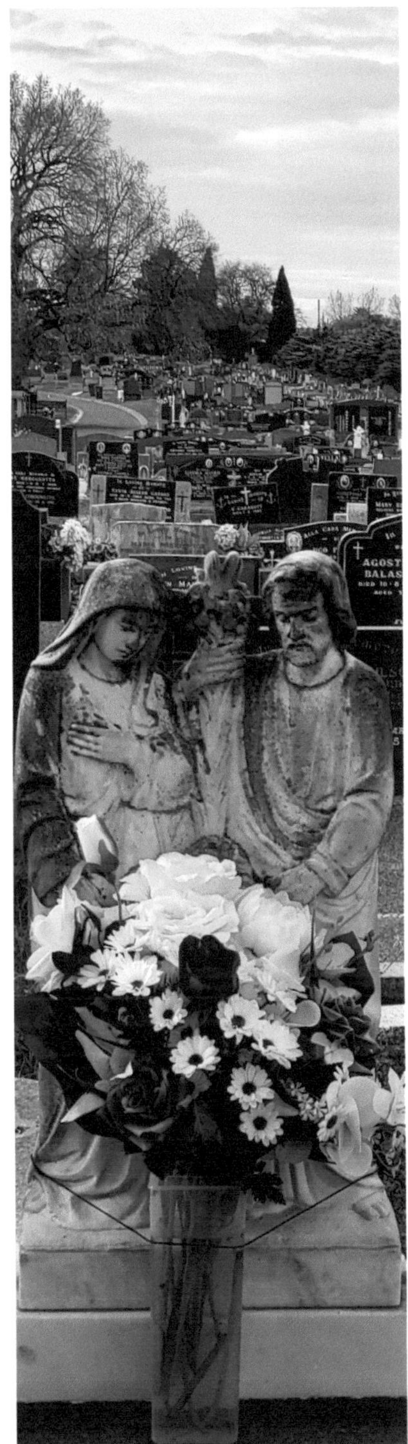
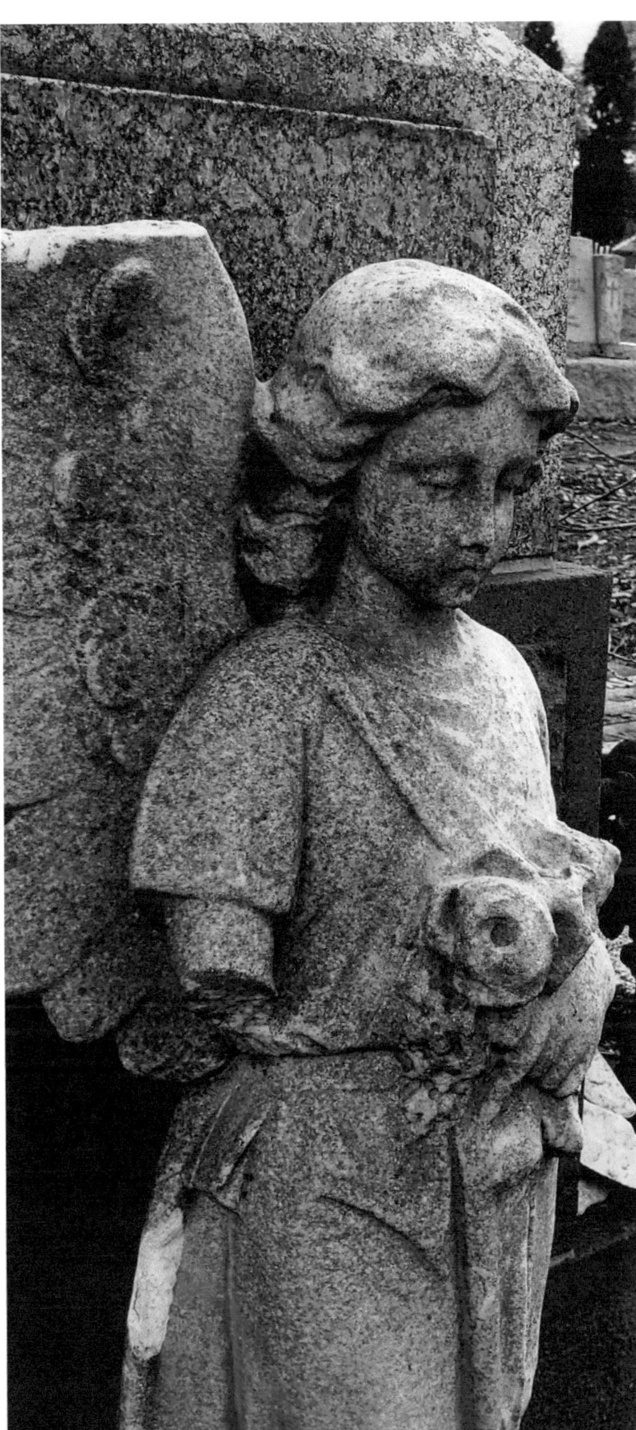
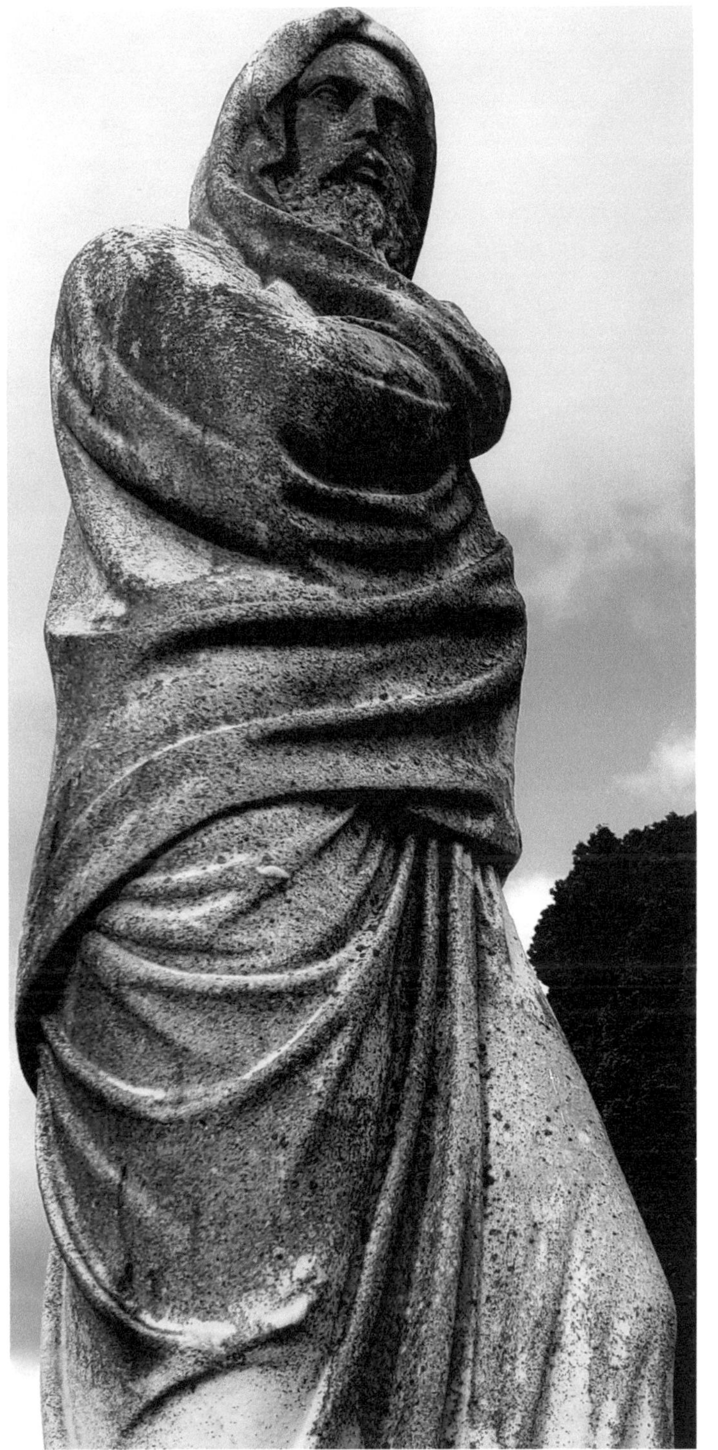

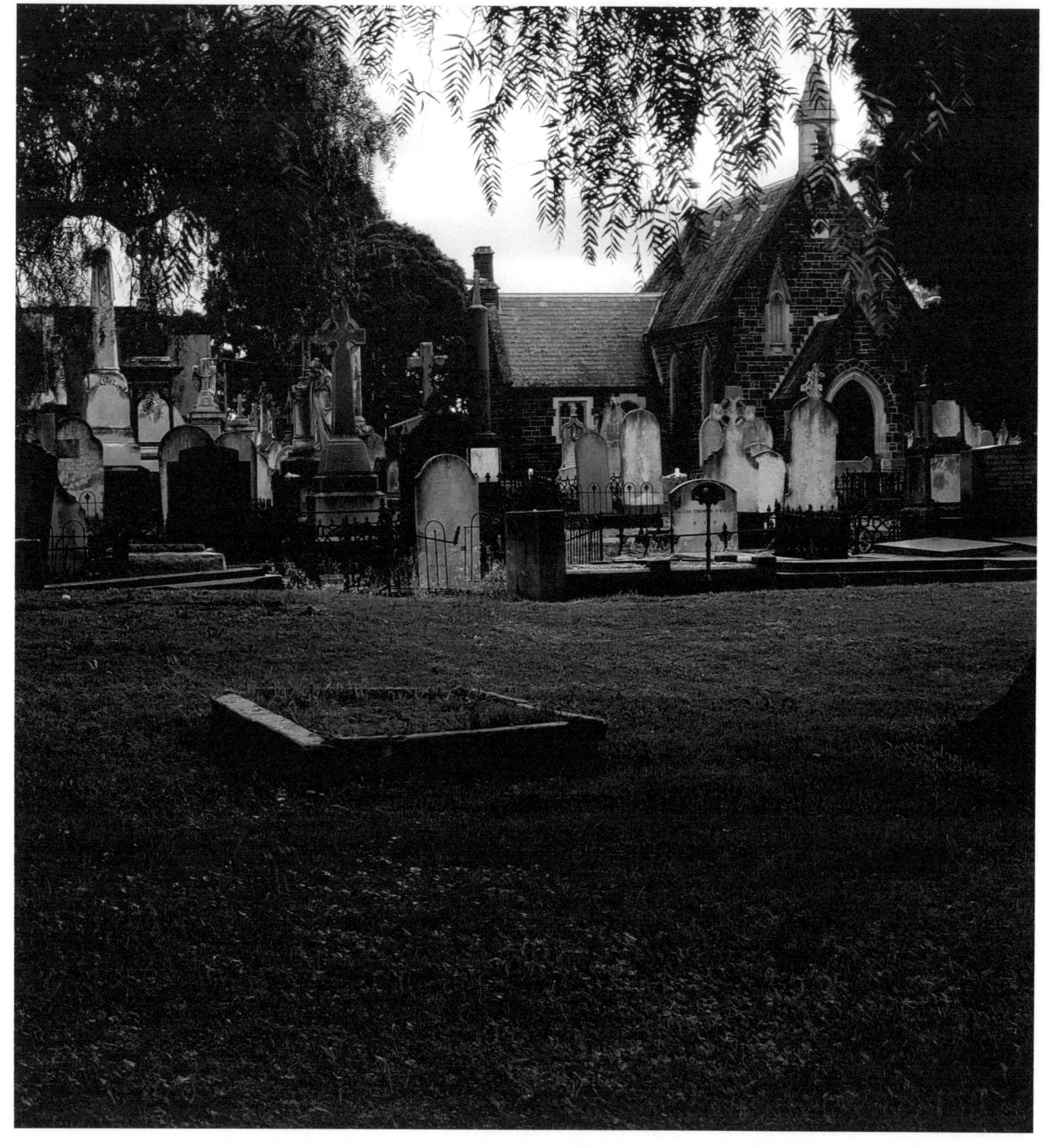

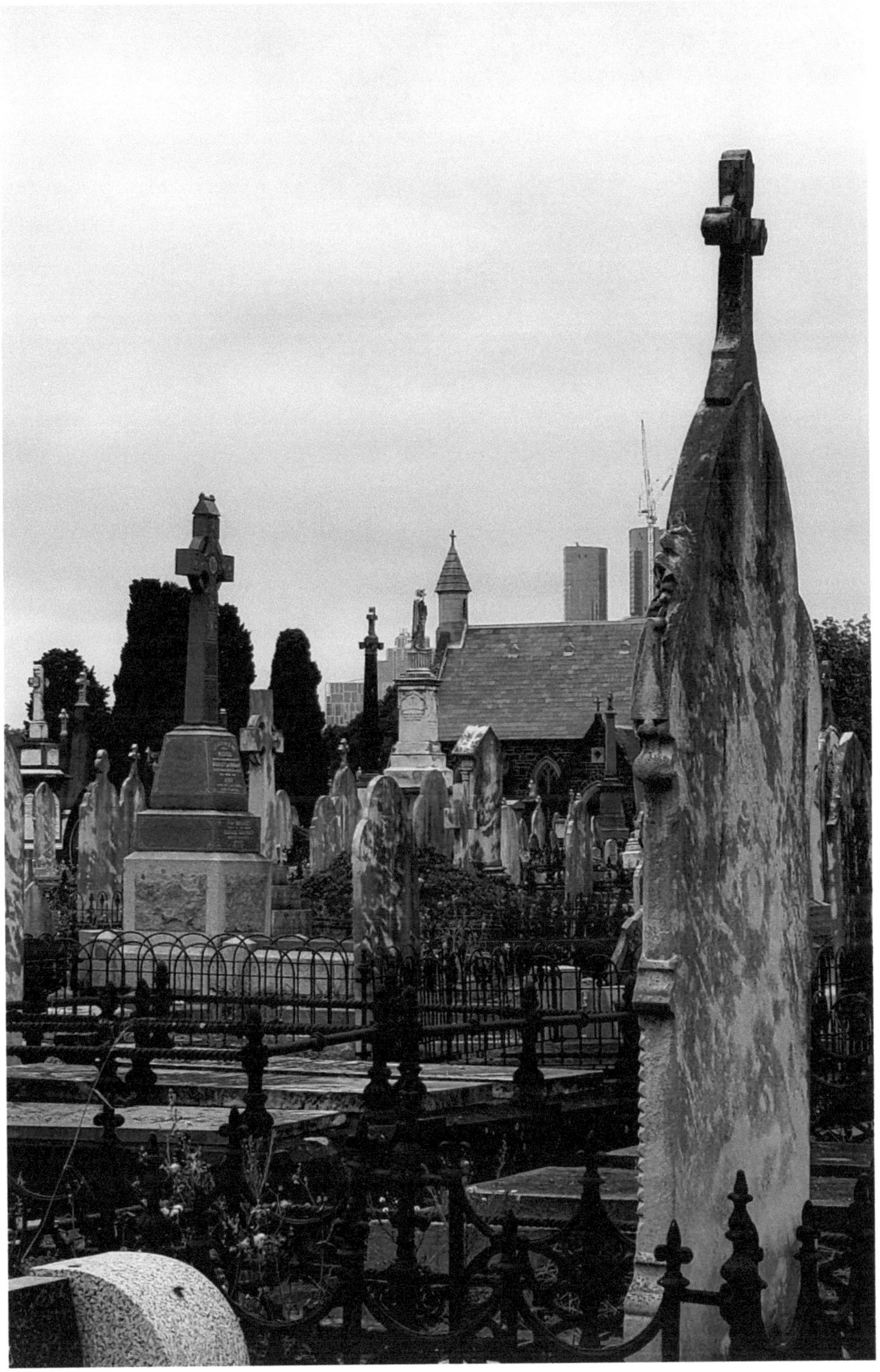

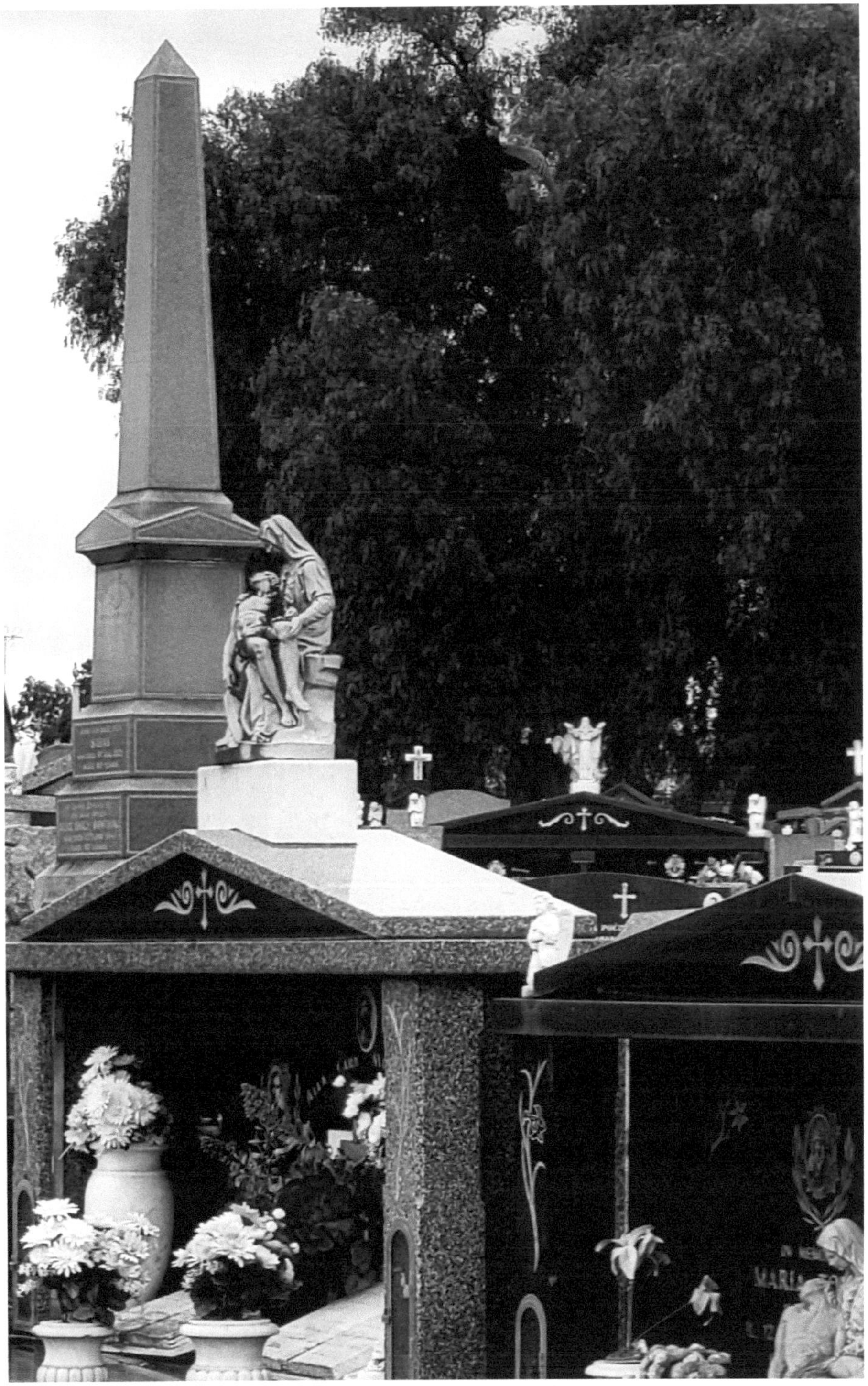

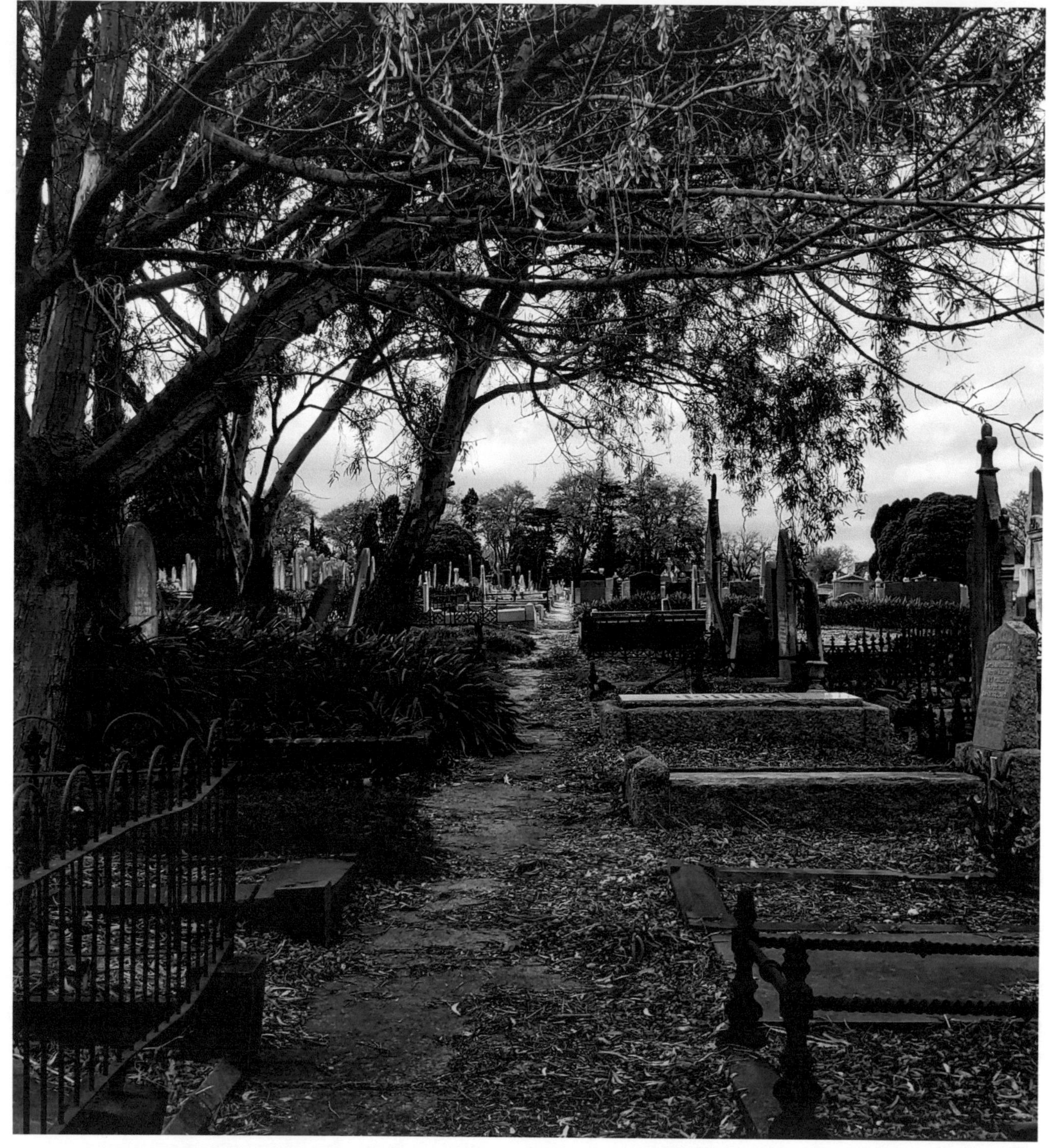

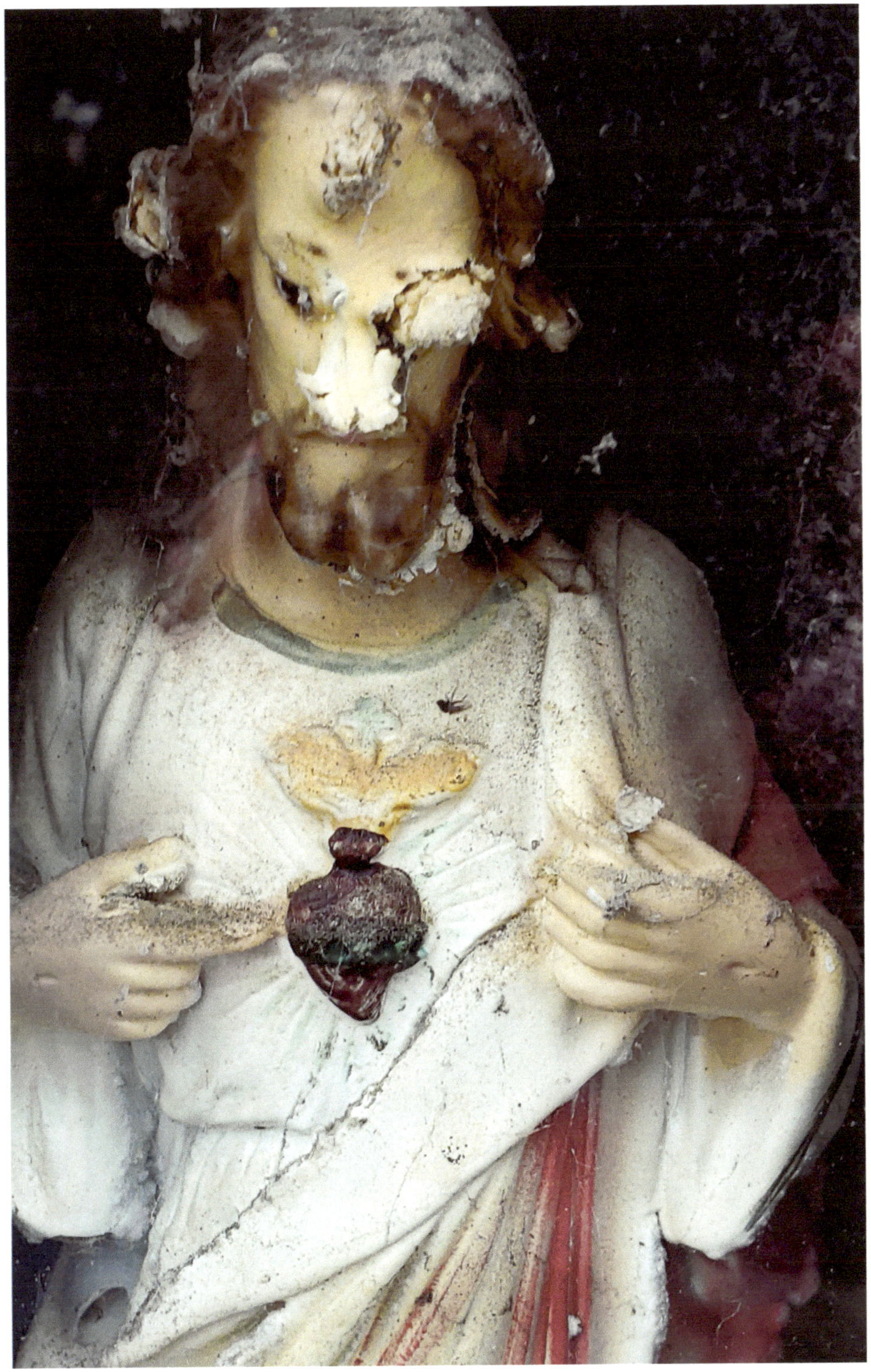

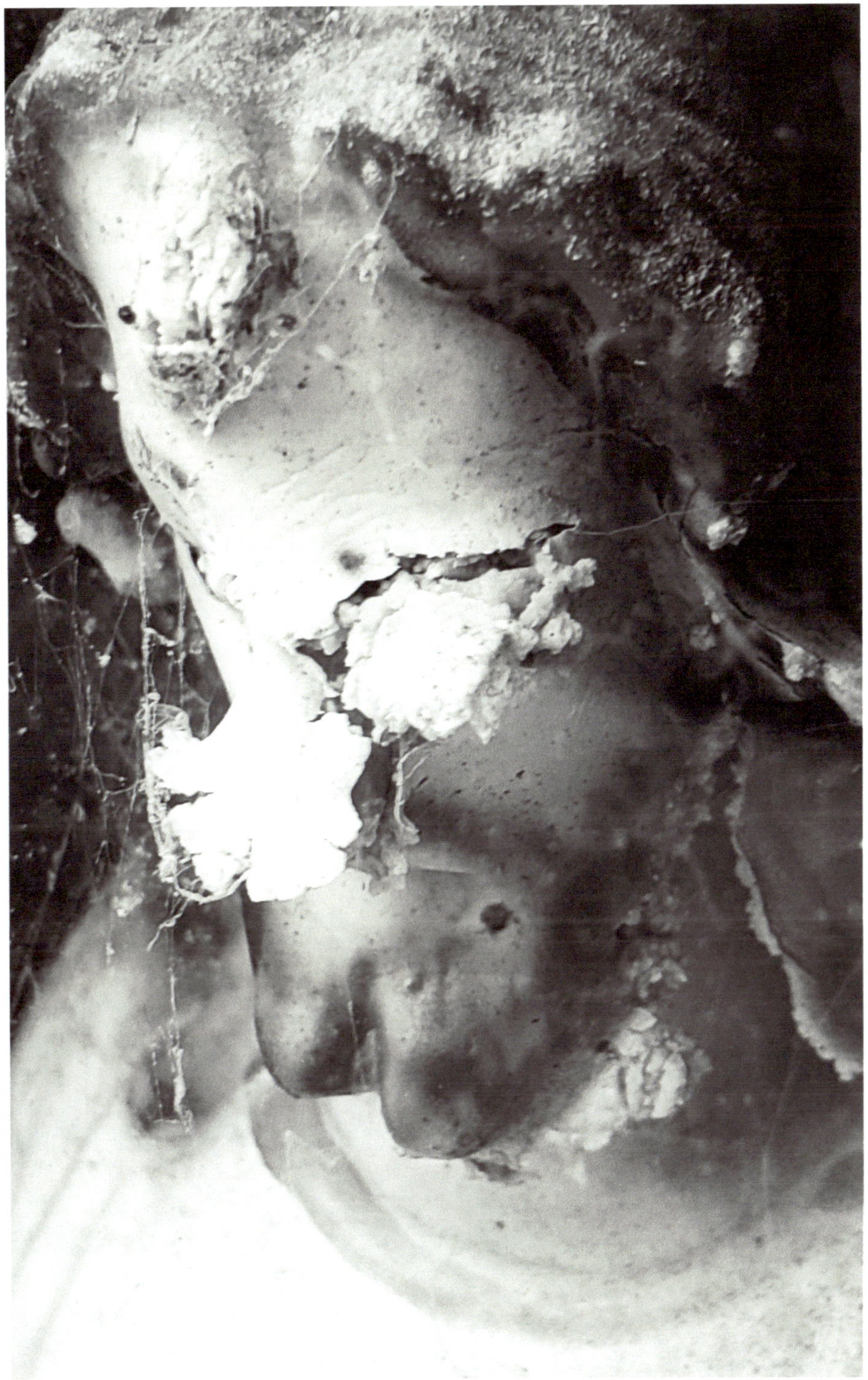

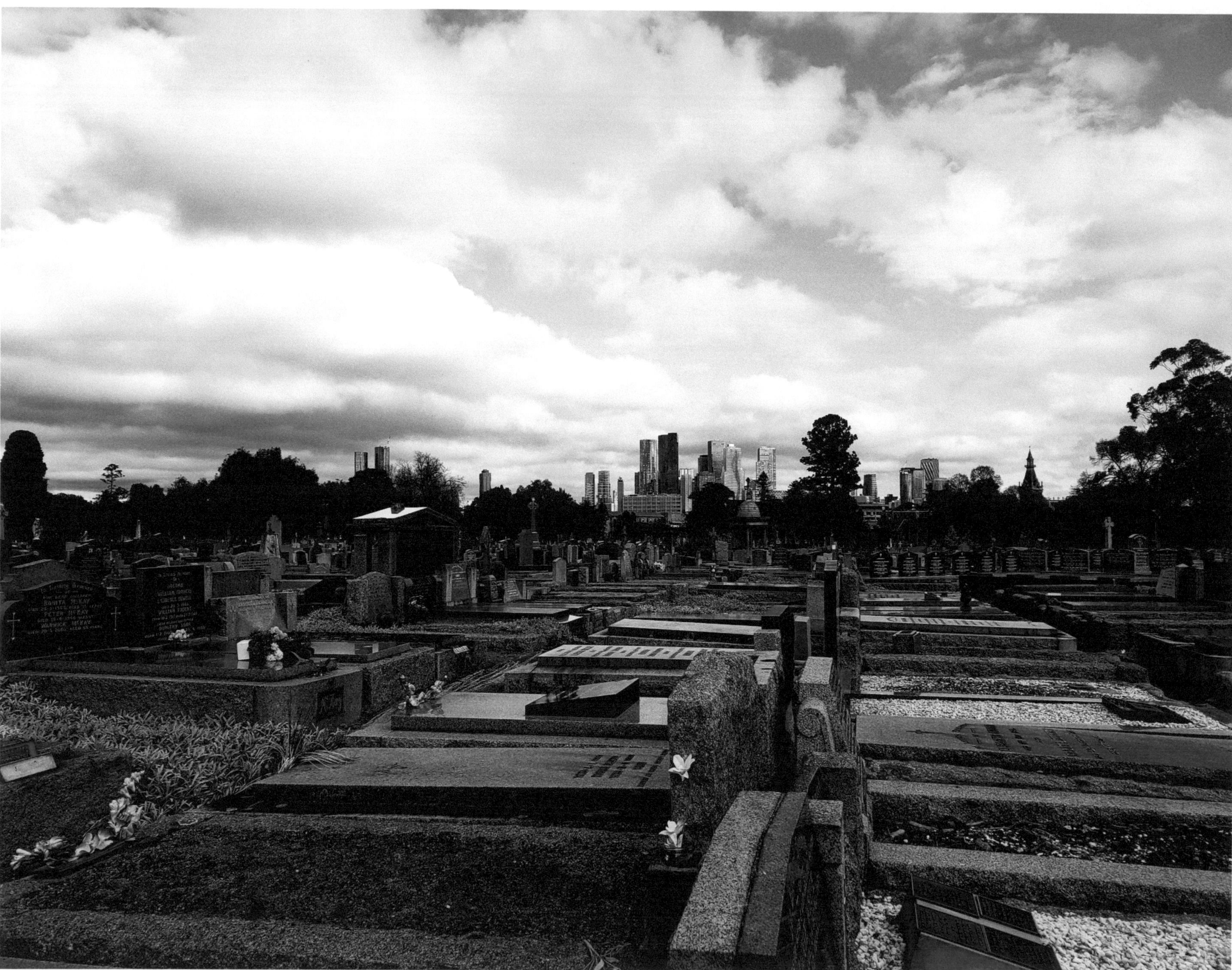

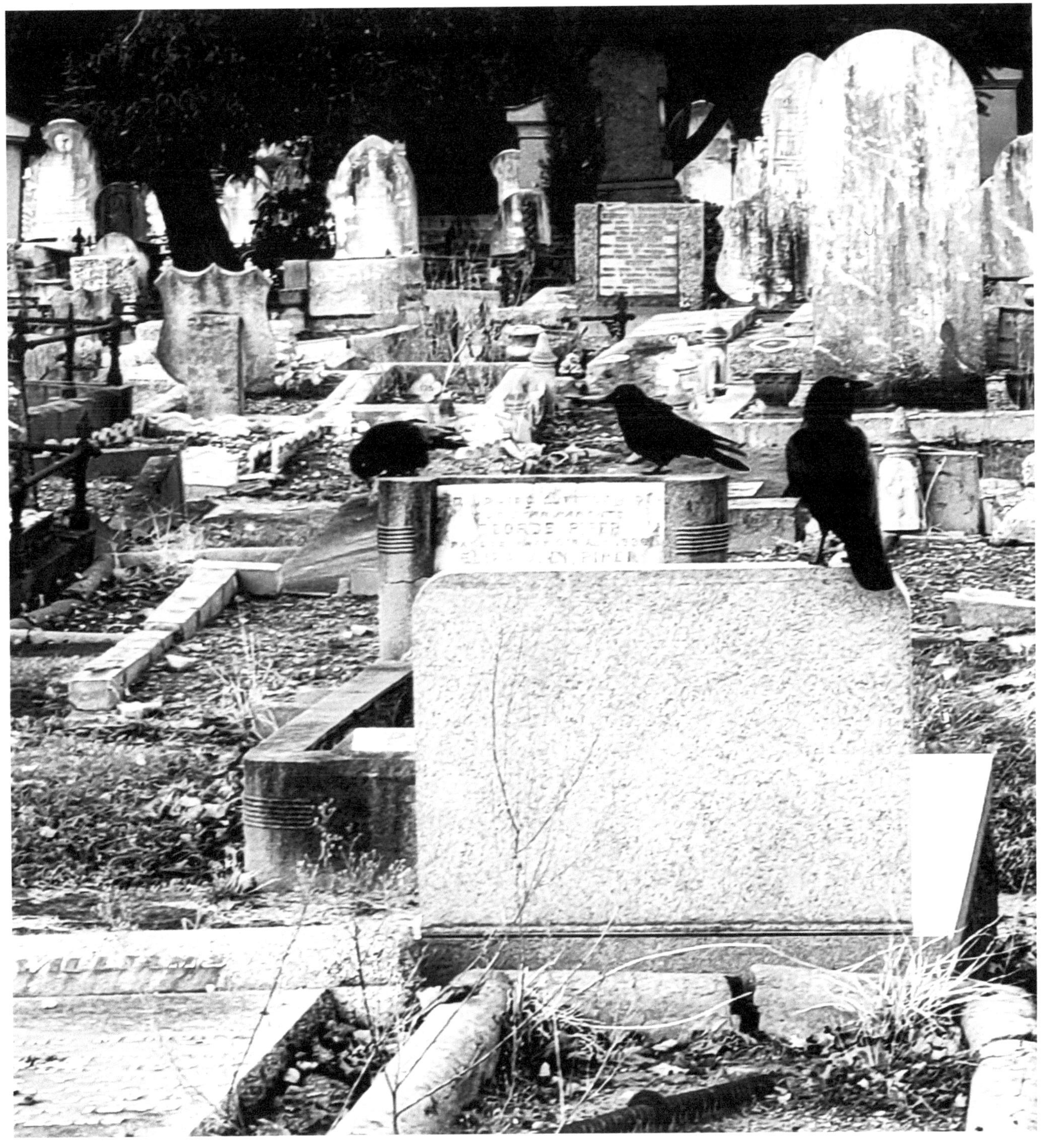

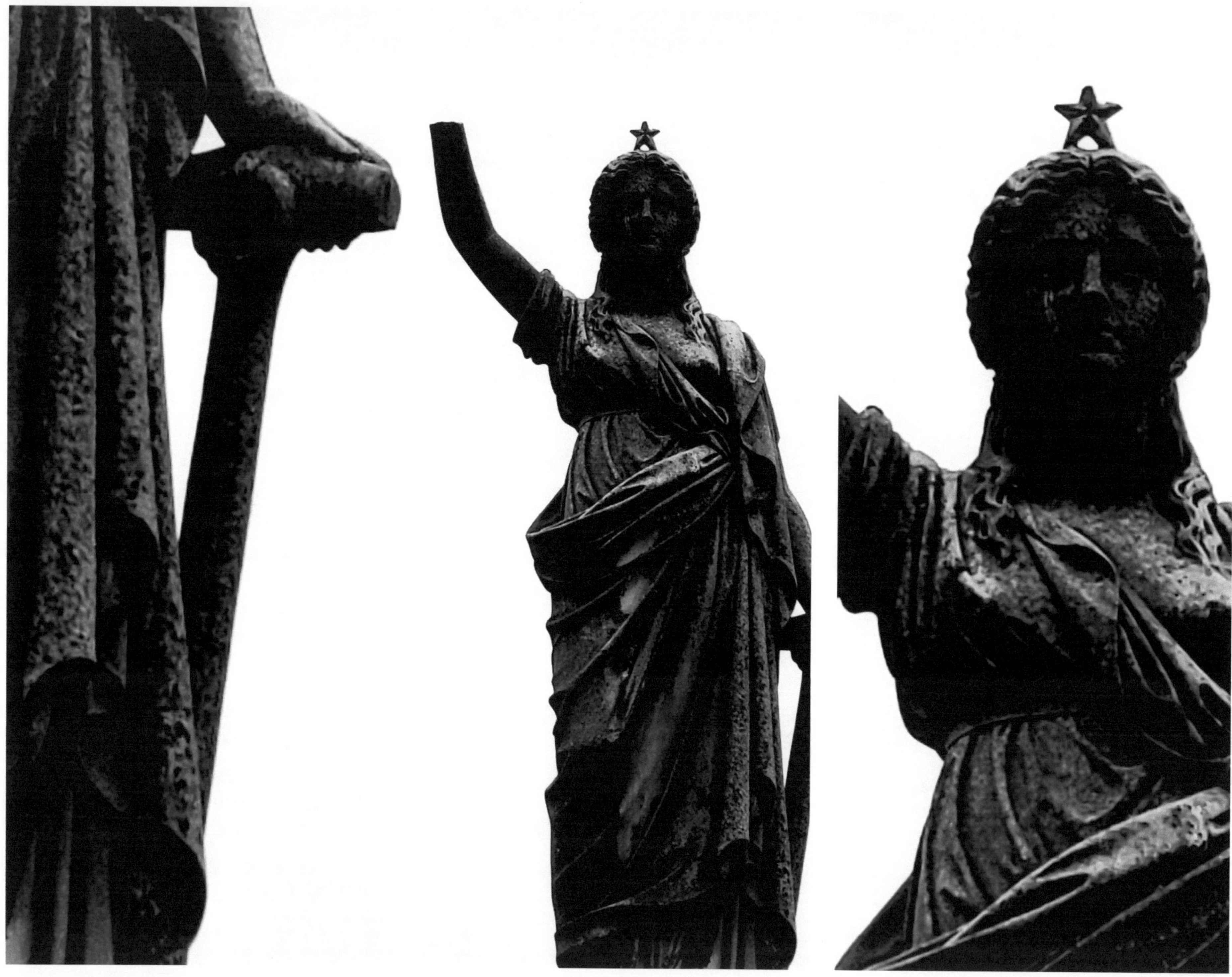

Preston Cemetery

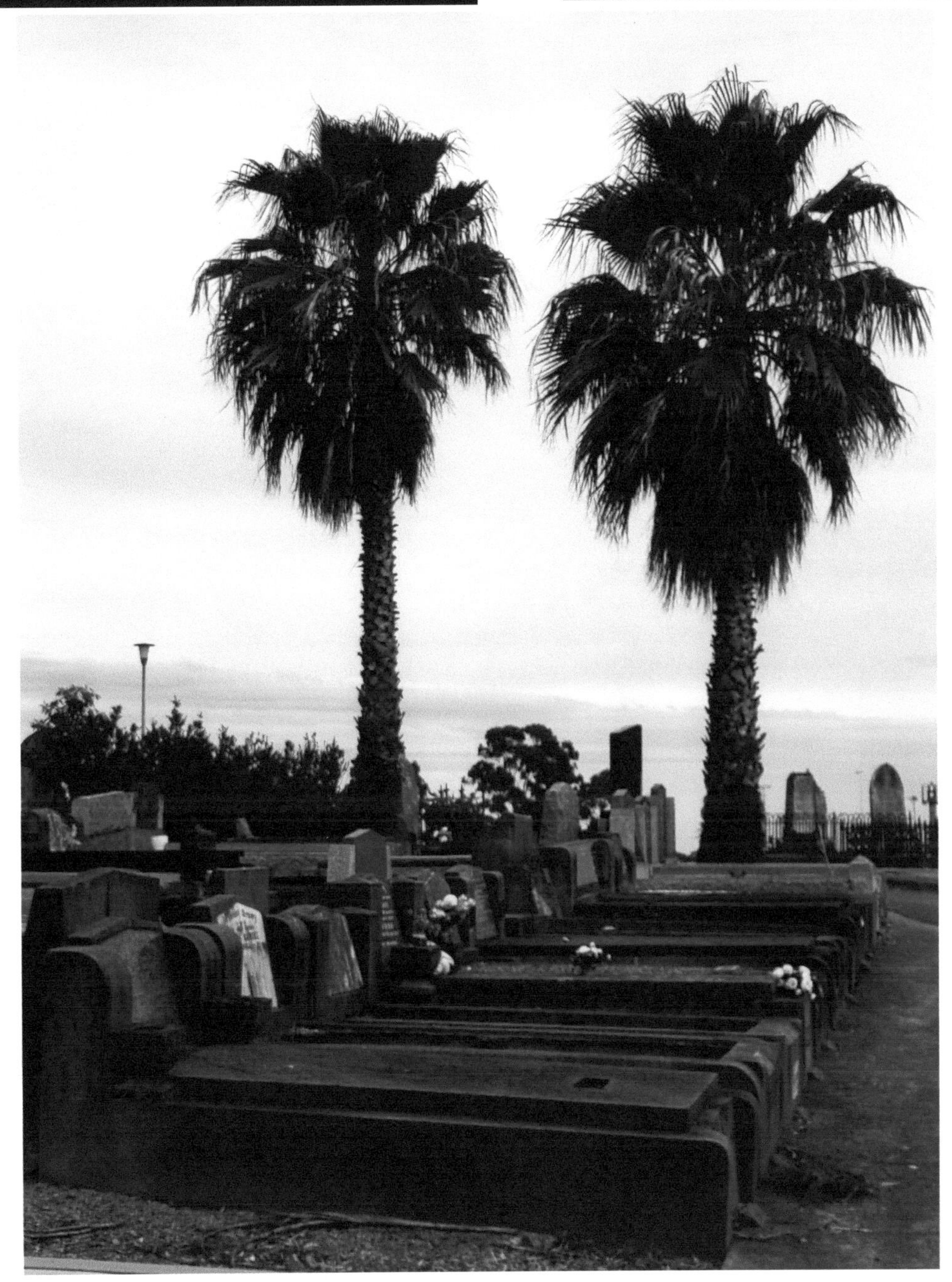

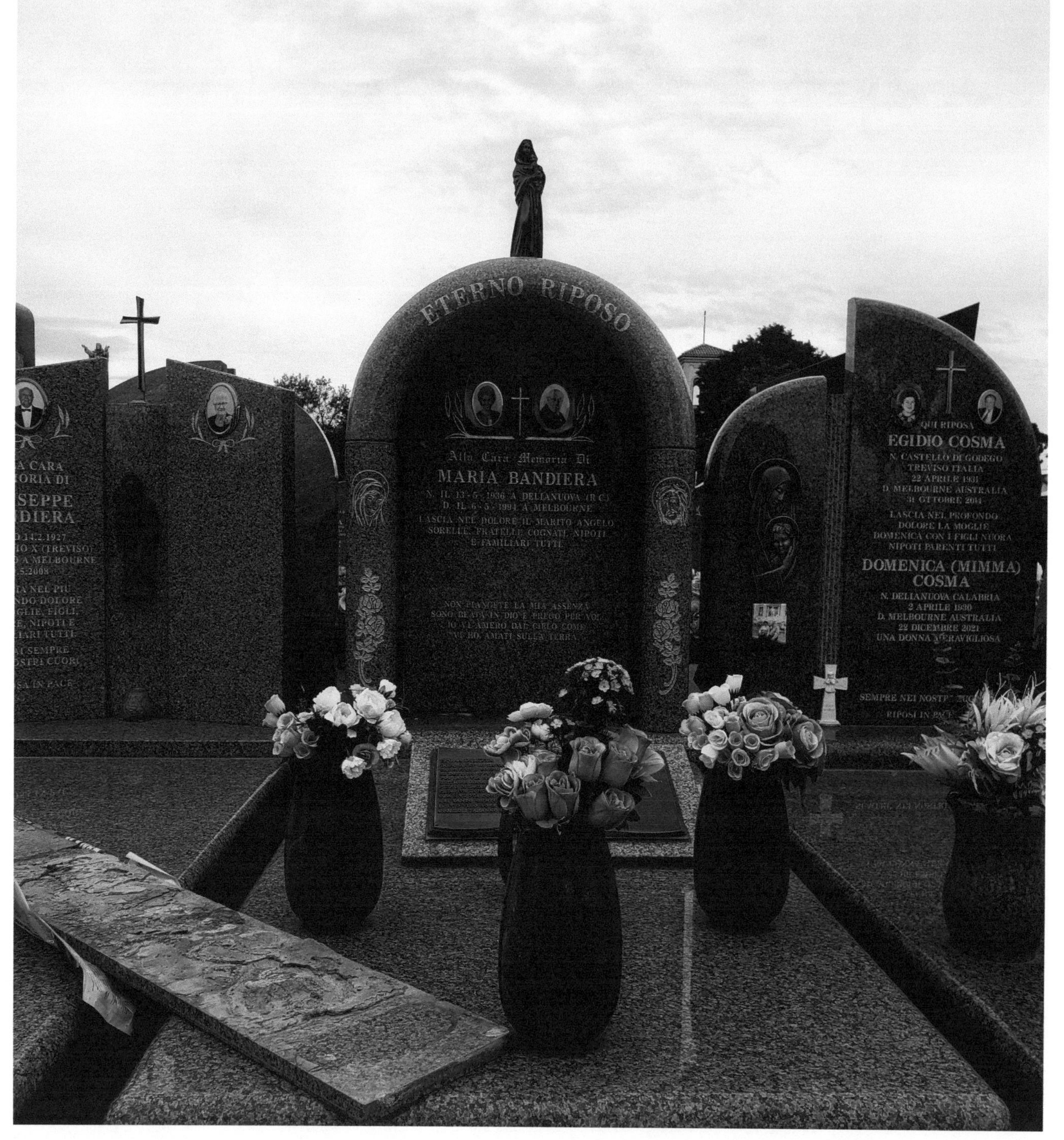

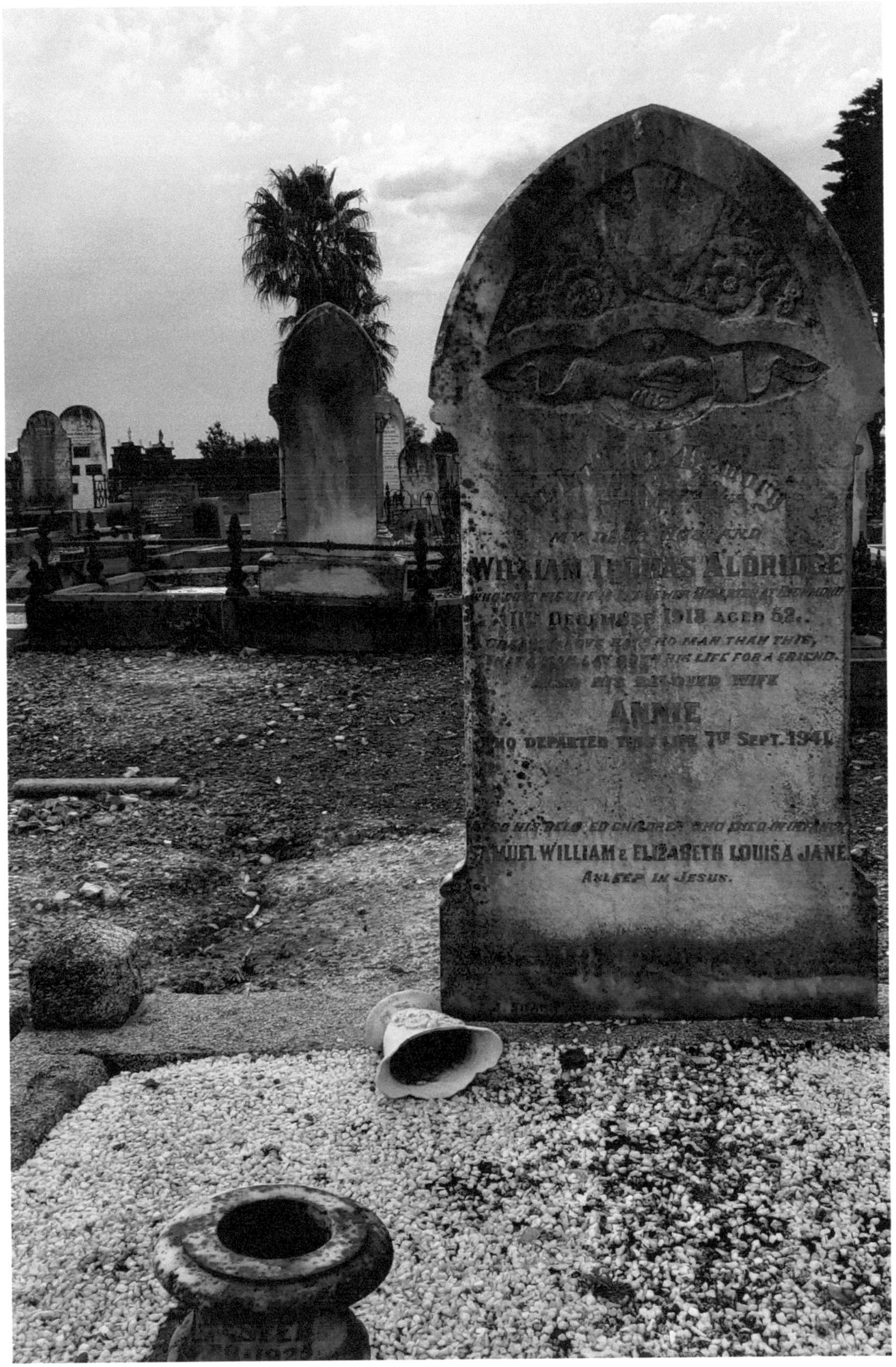

MY DEAR HUSBAND
WILLIAM THOMAS ALDRIDGE
WHO LOST HIS LIFE IN A MOTOR DISASTER AT BORDERTOWN
11TH DECEMBER 1918 AGED 52.
GREATER LOVE HATH NO MAN THAN THIS,
THAT A MAN LAY DOWN HIS LIFE FOR A FRIEND.
ALSO HIS BELOVED WIFE
ANNIE
WHO DEPARTED THIS LIFE 7TH SEPT. 1941
ALSO HIS BELOVED CHILDREN WHO DIED IN INFANCY
SAMUEL WILLIAM & ELIZABETH LOUISA JANE
ASLEEP IN JESUS.

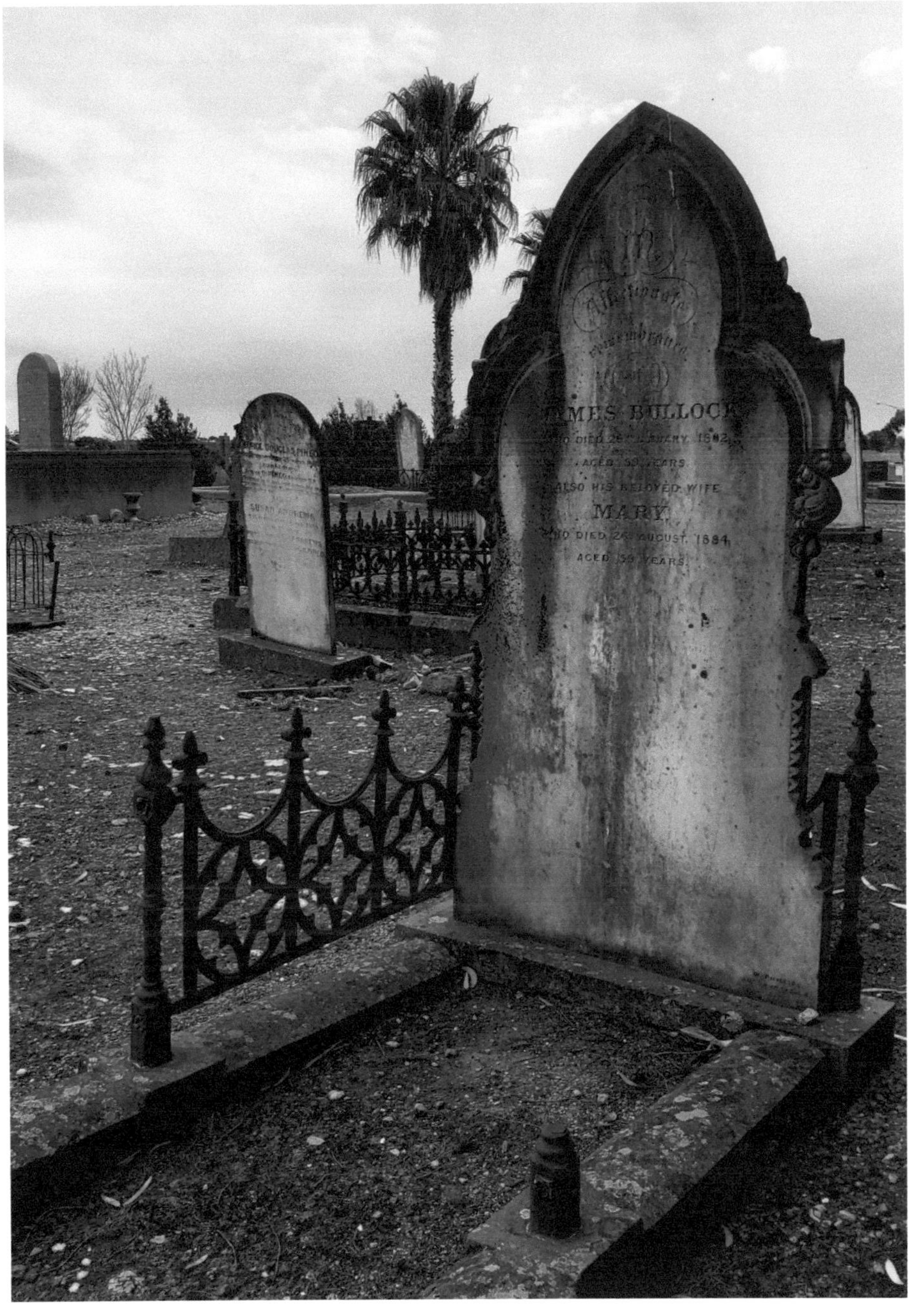

In
Affectionate
Remembrance
of
JAMES BULLOCK
WHO DIED 26 JANUARY 1882,
AGED 59 YEARS
ALSO HIS BELOVED WIFE
MARY
WHO DIED 24 AUGUST 1884,
AGED 59 YEARS

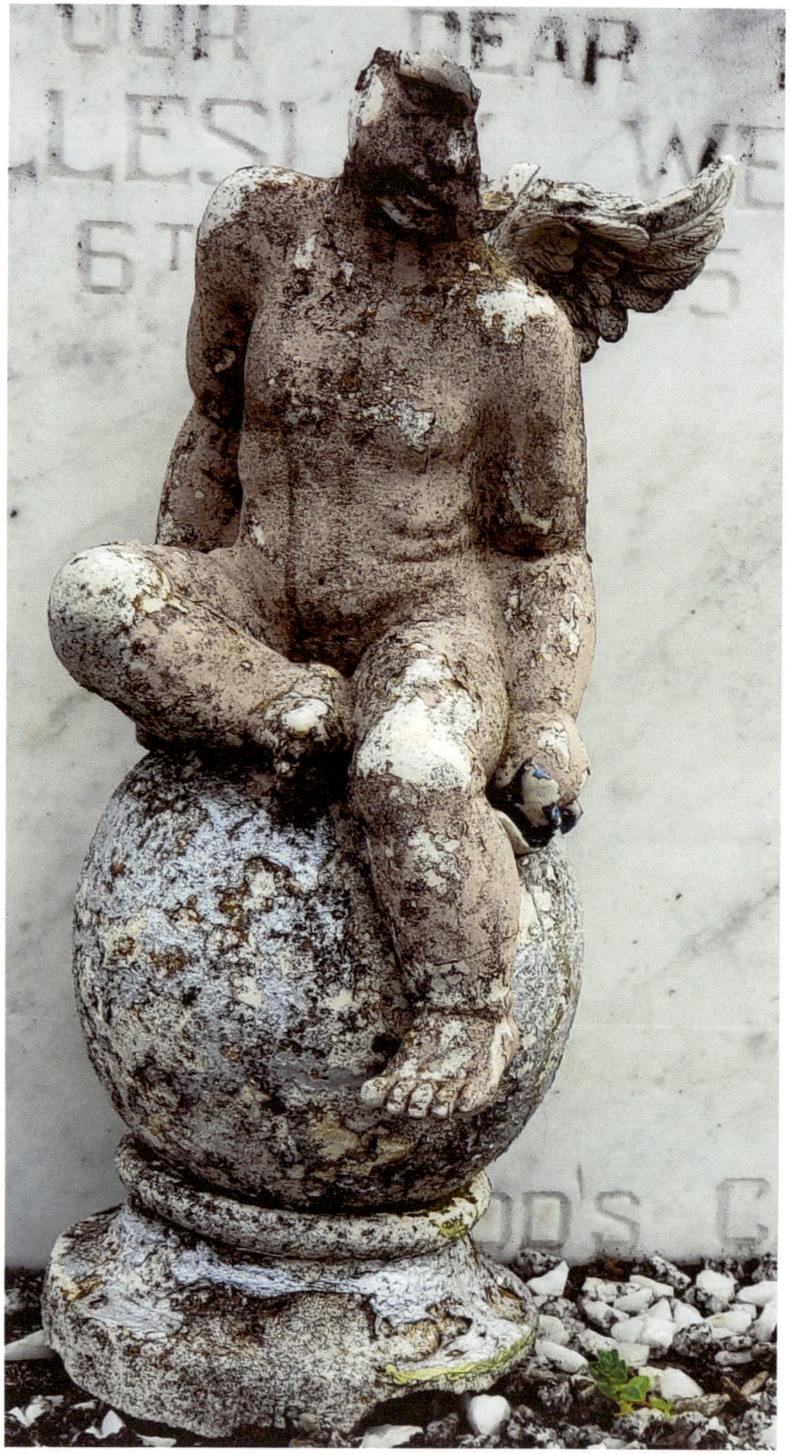

OUR DEAR
LESL   WE
6T
OOD'S G

In Loving Memory Of
MY LOVED HUSBAND
& OUR DEAR FATHER
FRANCIS HUGH
1988
MOTHER
ORIS

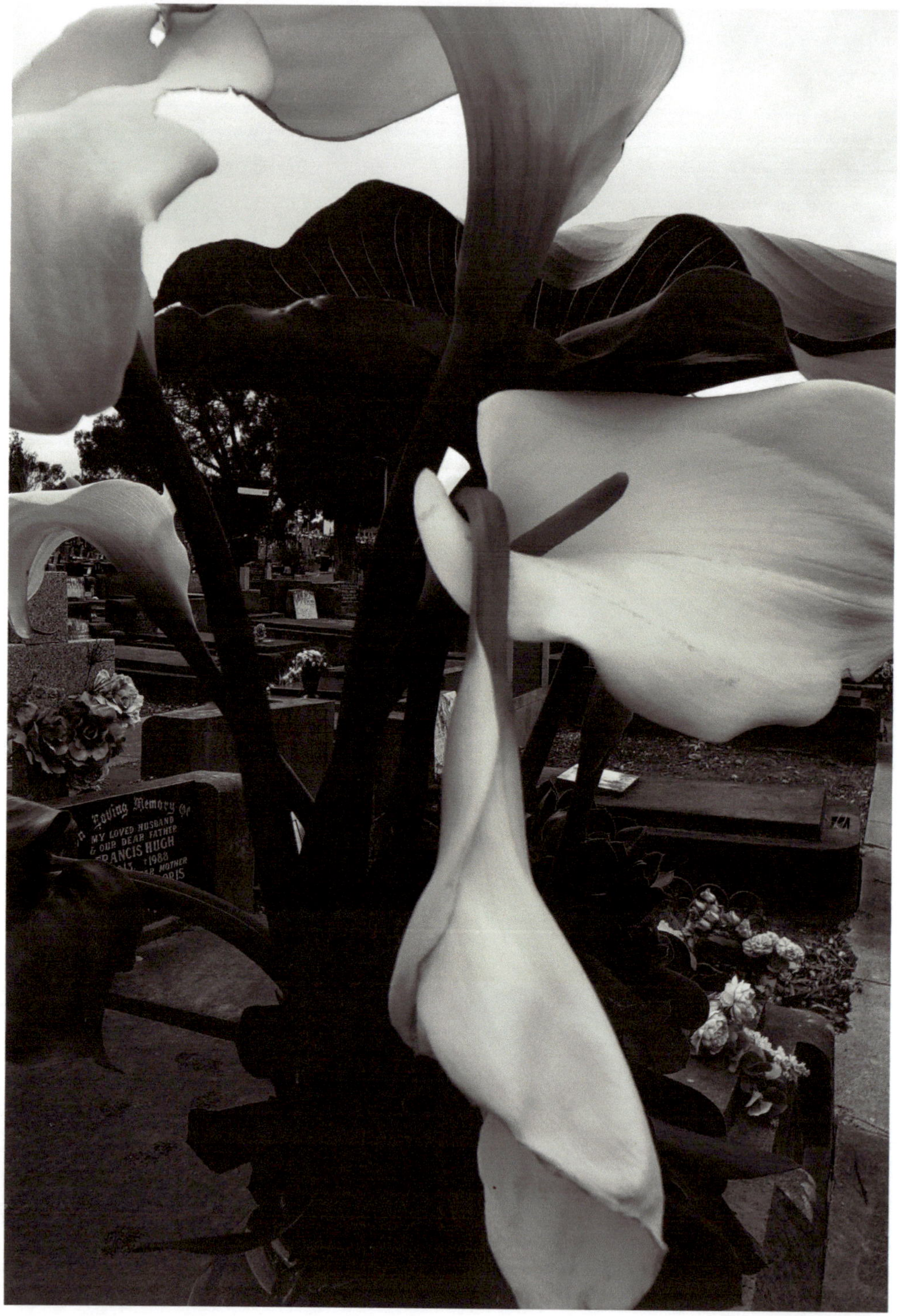

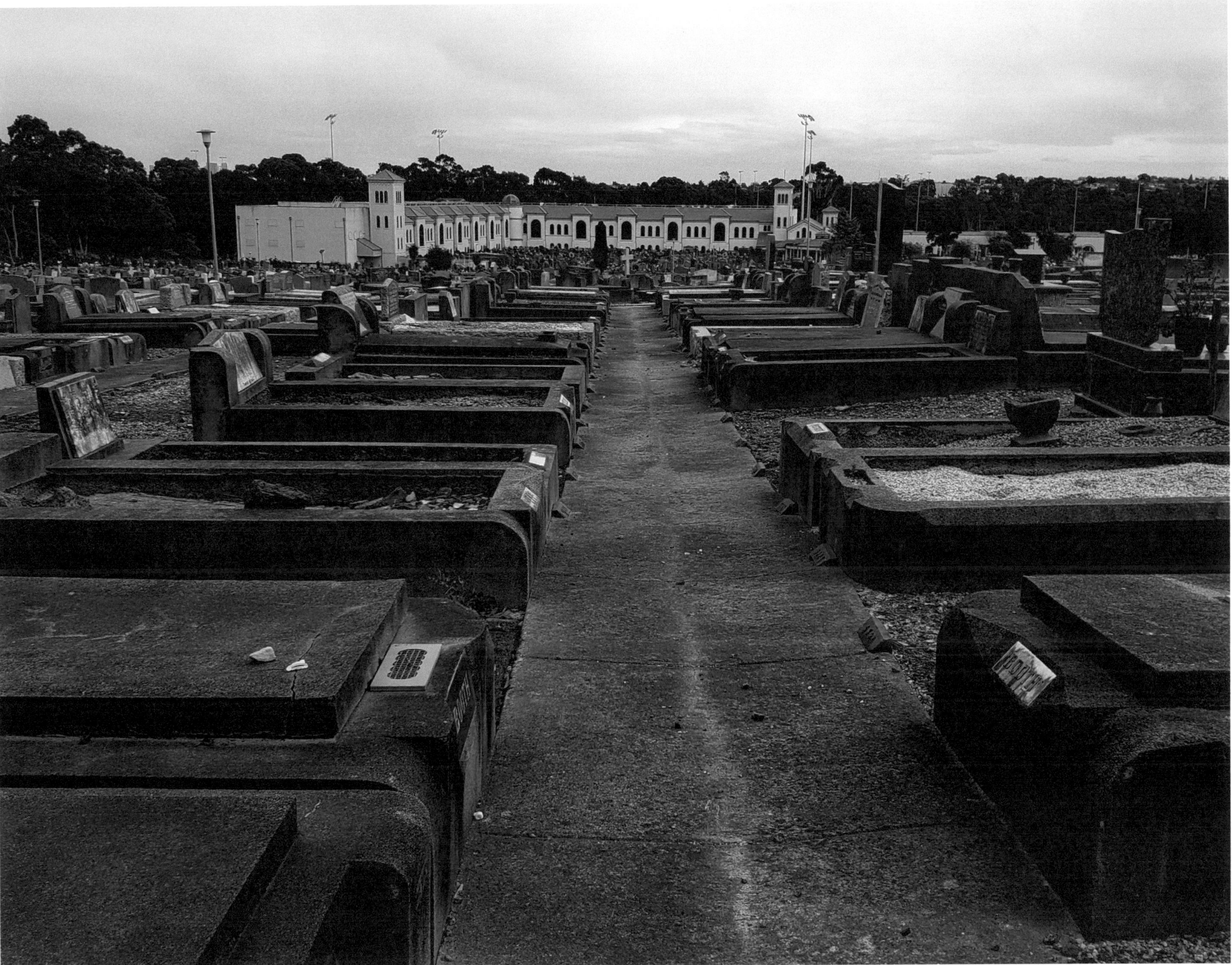

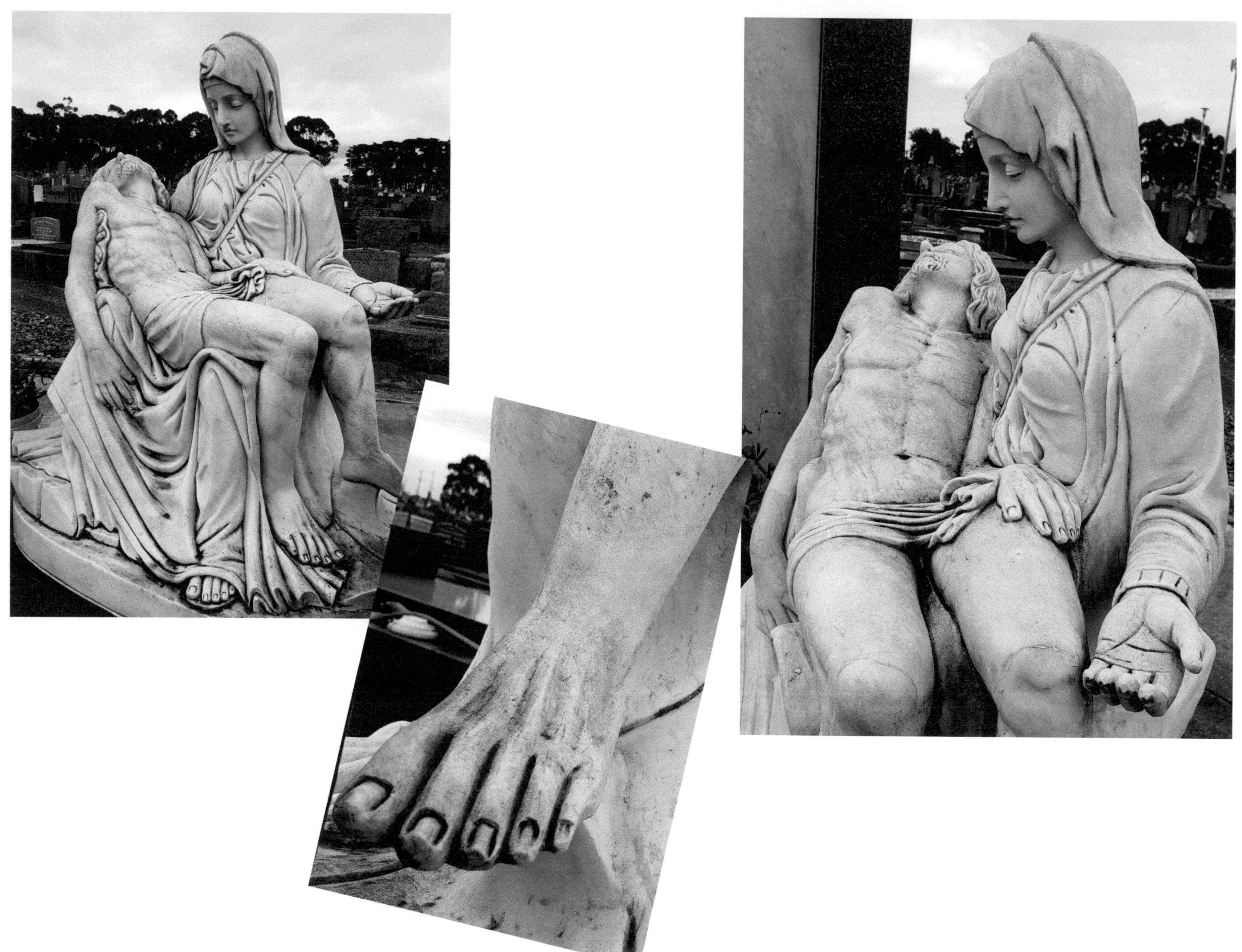

St. Kilda Cemetery

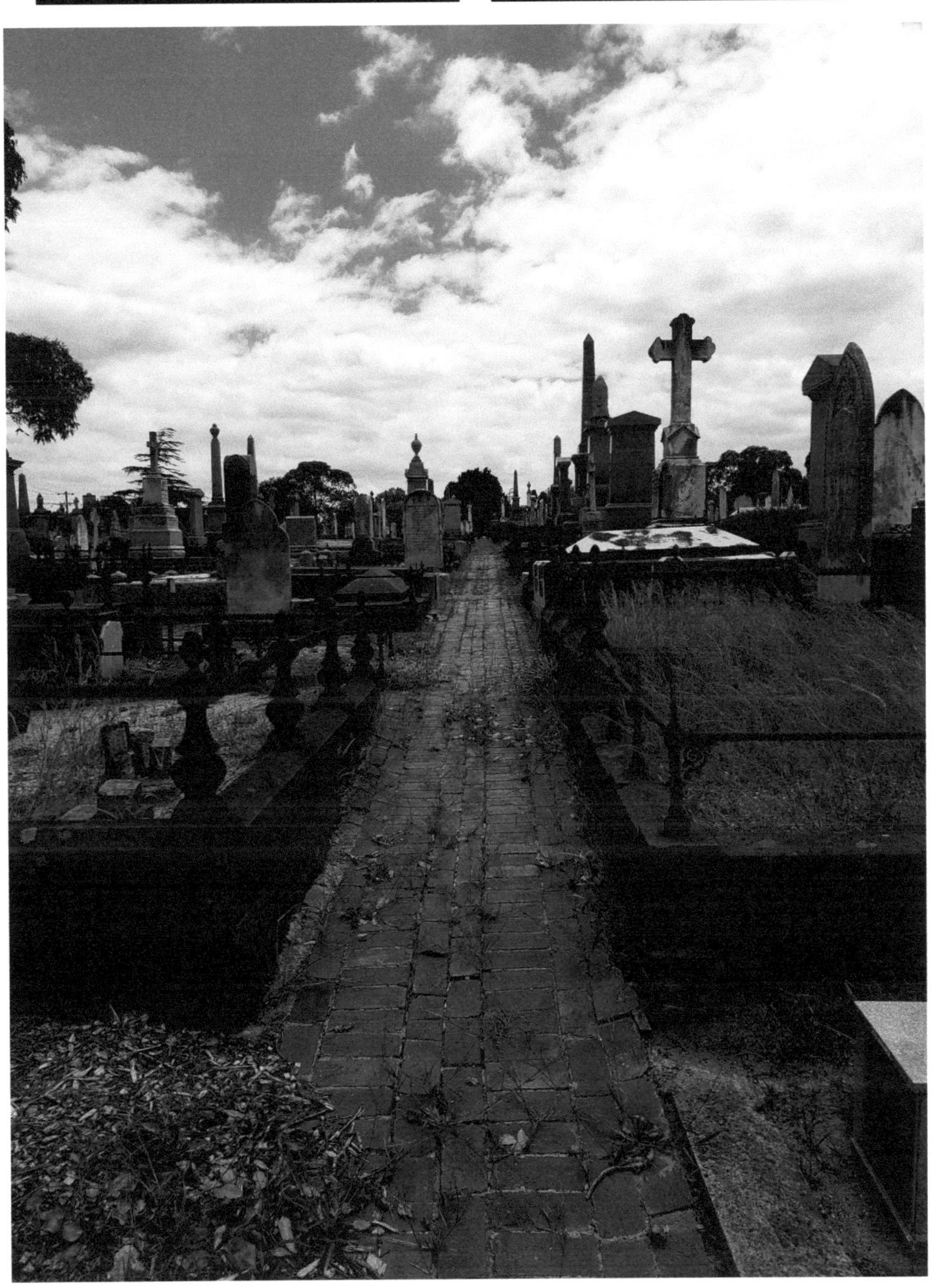

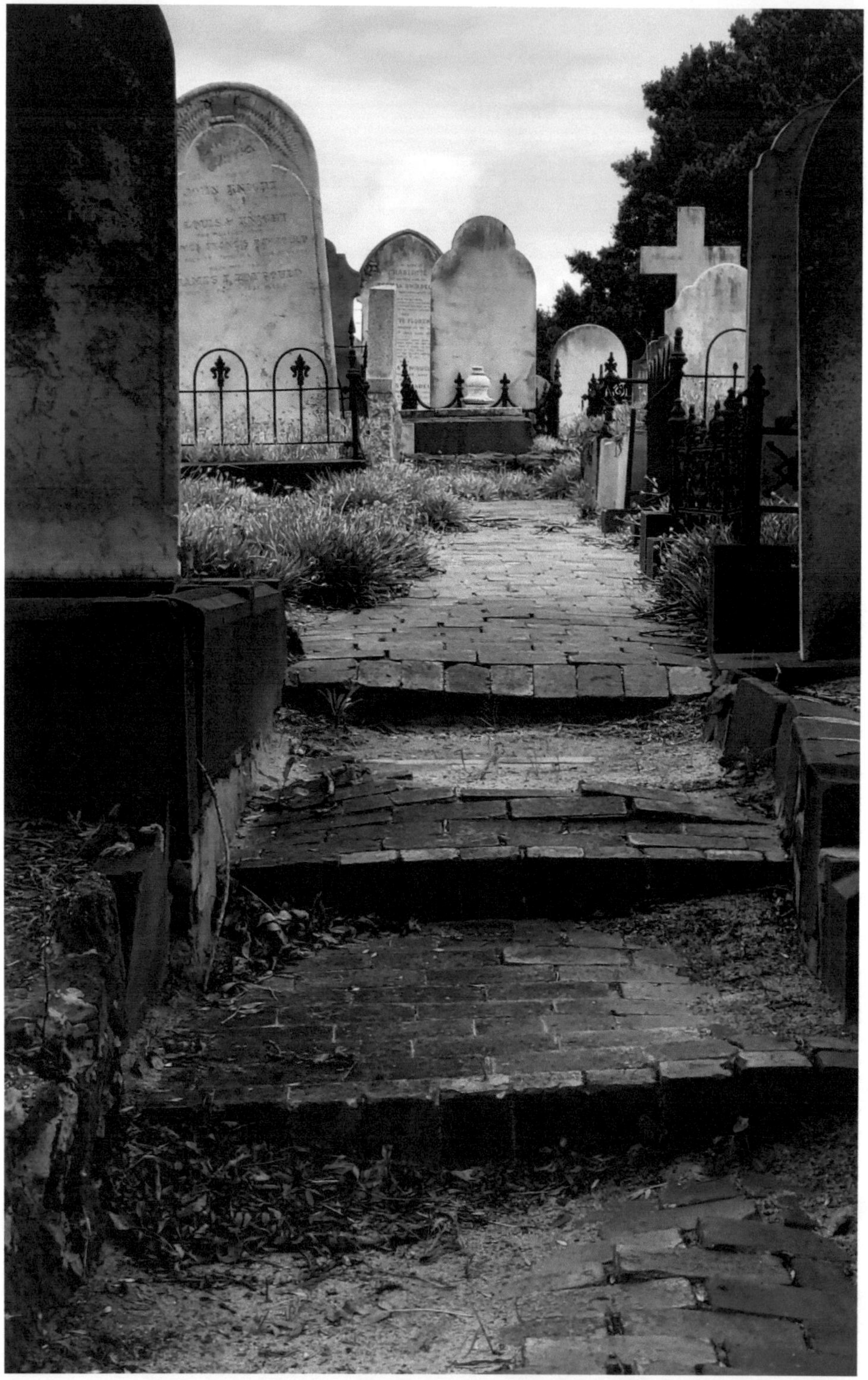

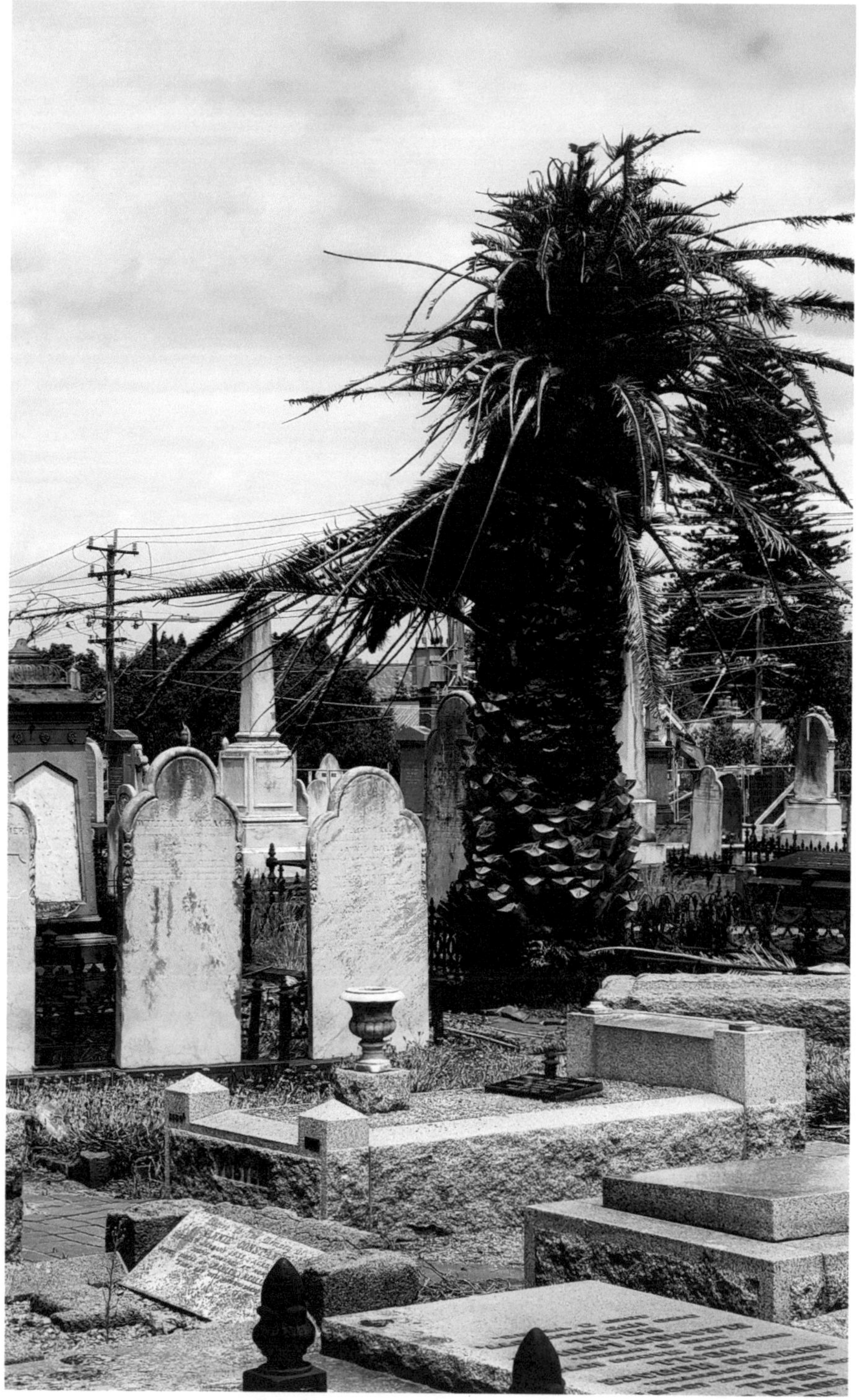

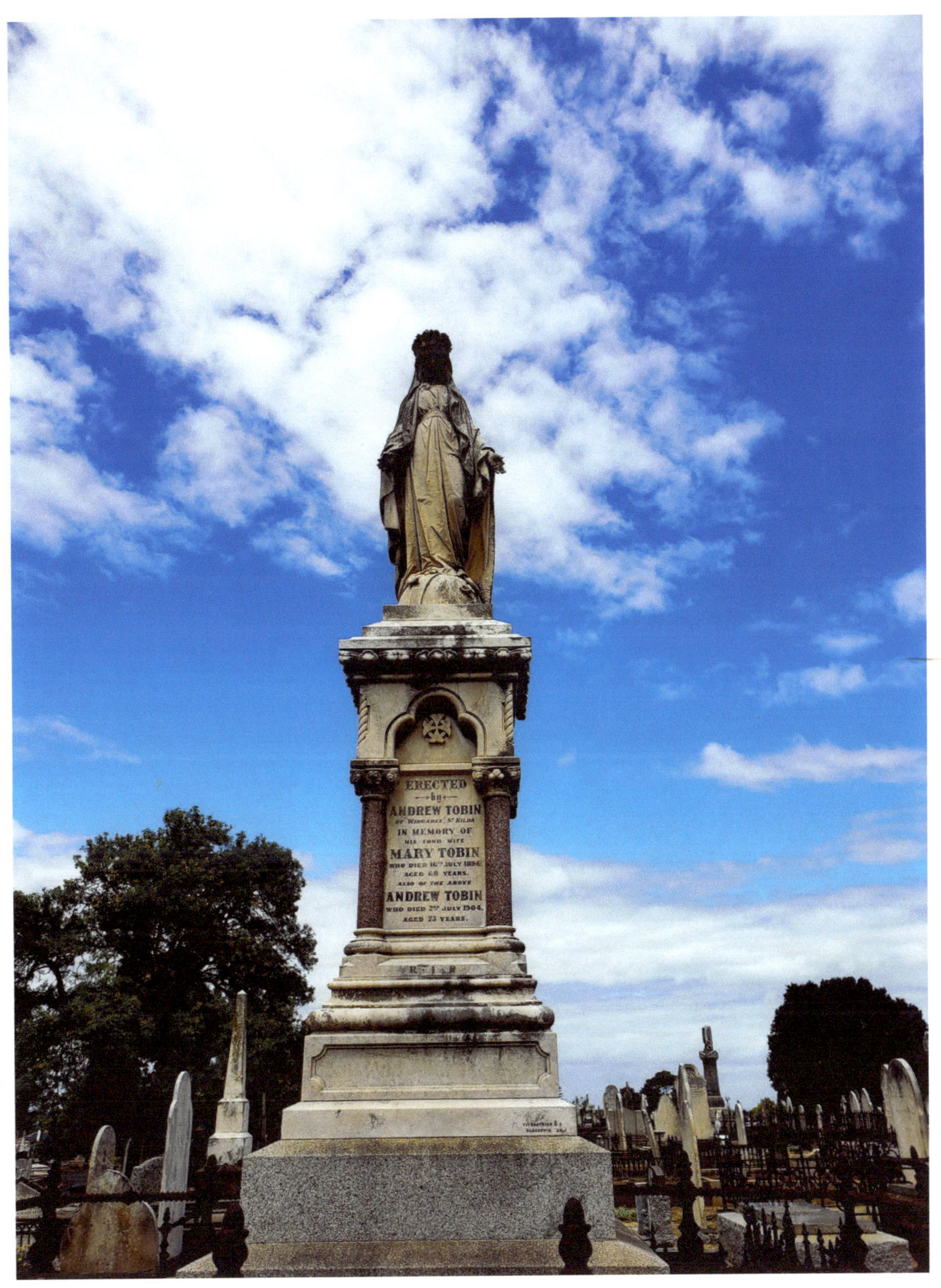

ERECTED
by
ANDREW TOBIN
OF WINGARIE, ST KILDA
IN MEMORY OF
HIS FOND WIFE
MARY TOBIN
WHO DIED 16TH JULY 1896
AGED 68 YEARS.
ALSO OF THE ABOVE
ANDREW TOBIN
WHO DIED 2ND JULY 1904,
AGED 73 YEARS.
R.I.P.

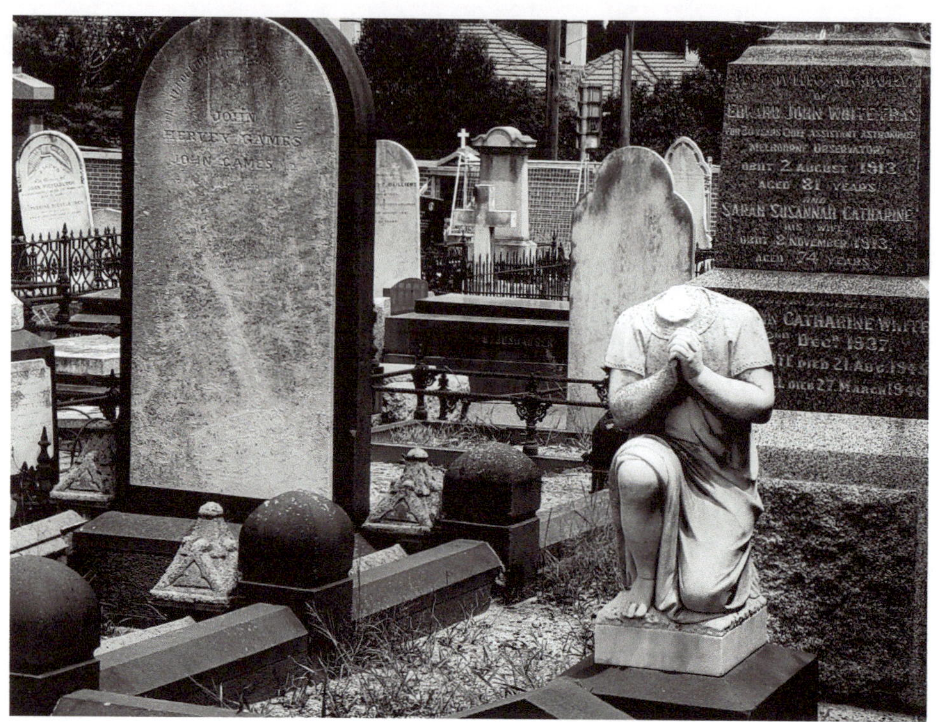
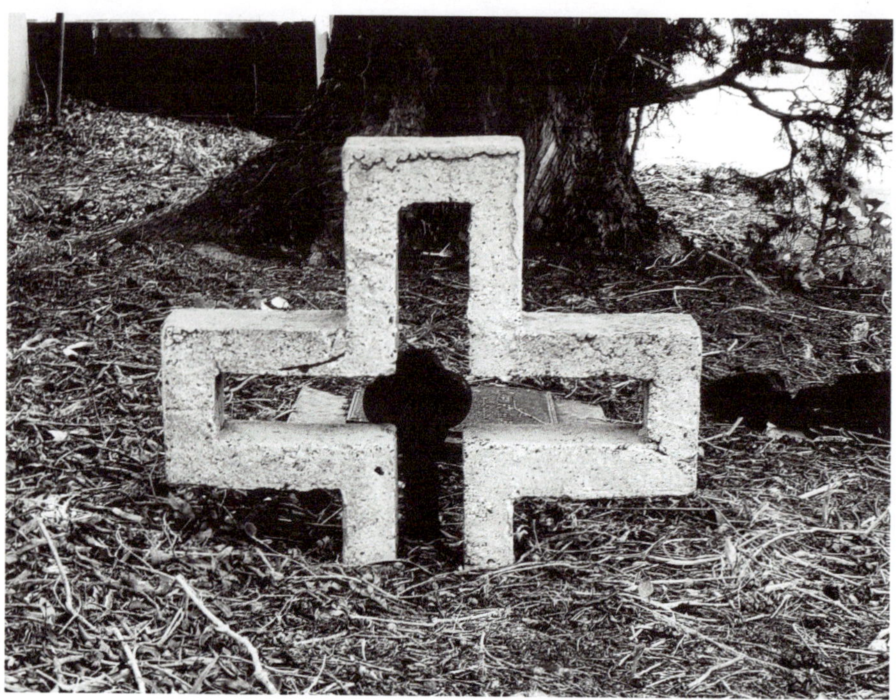

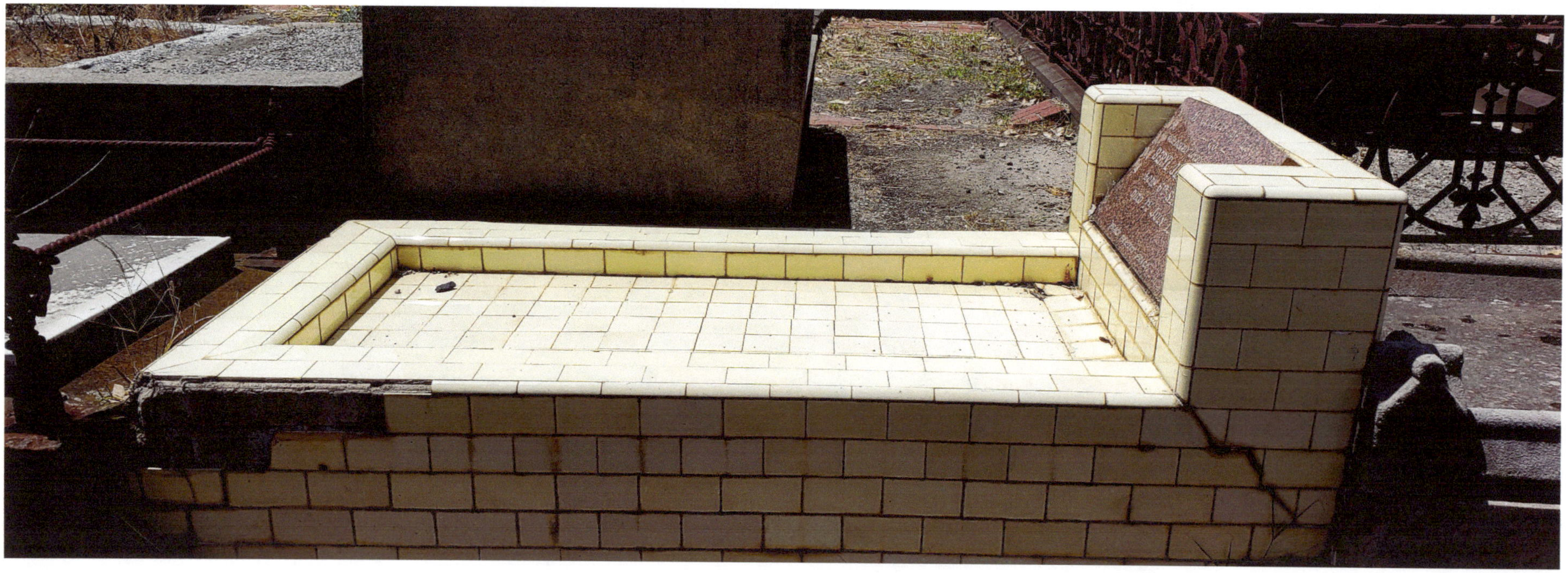

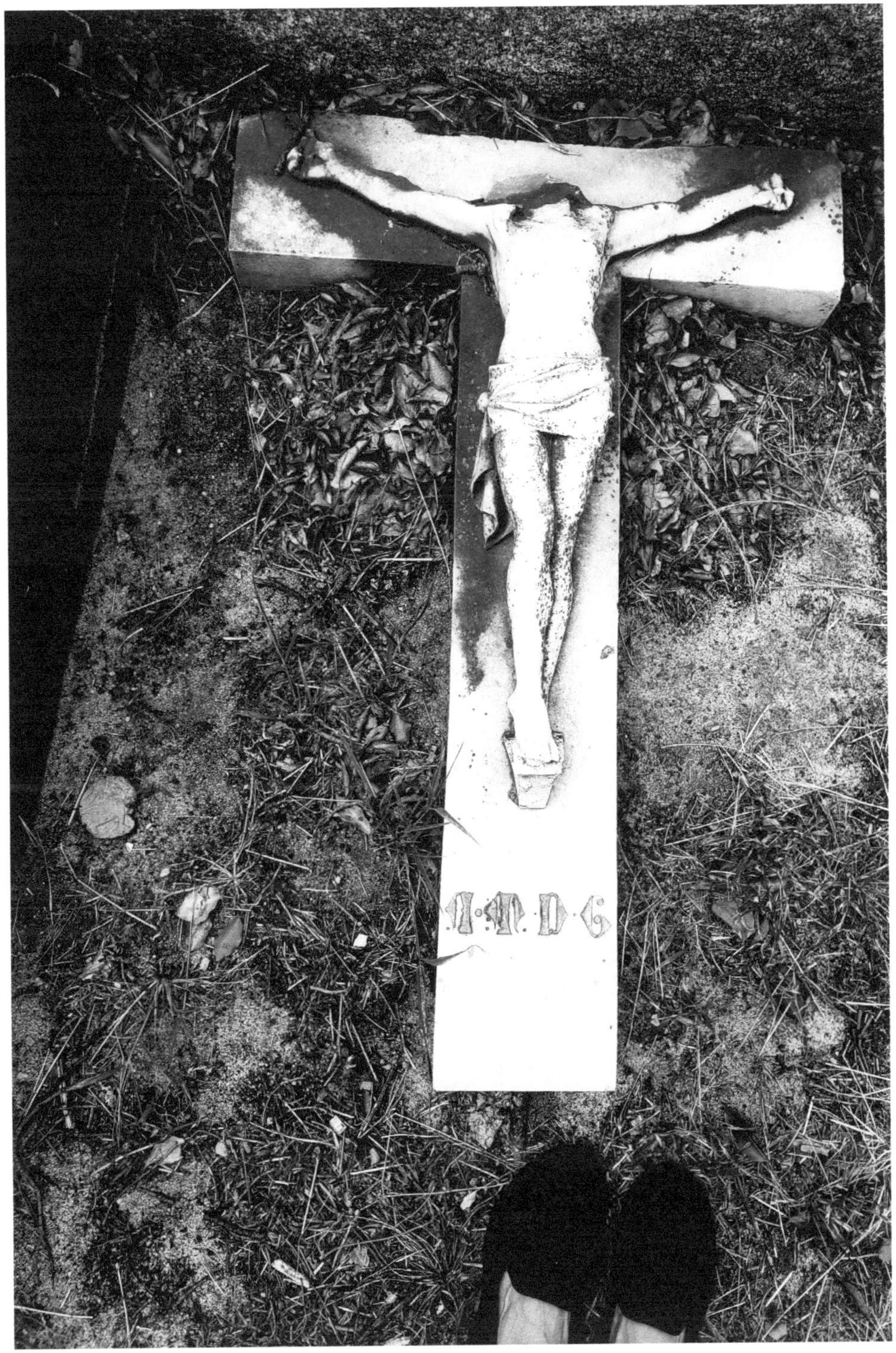

I.N.R.I.

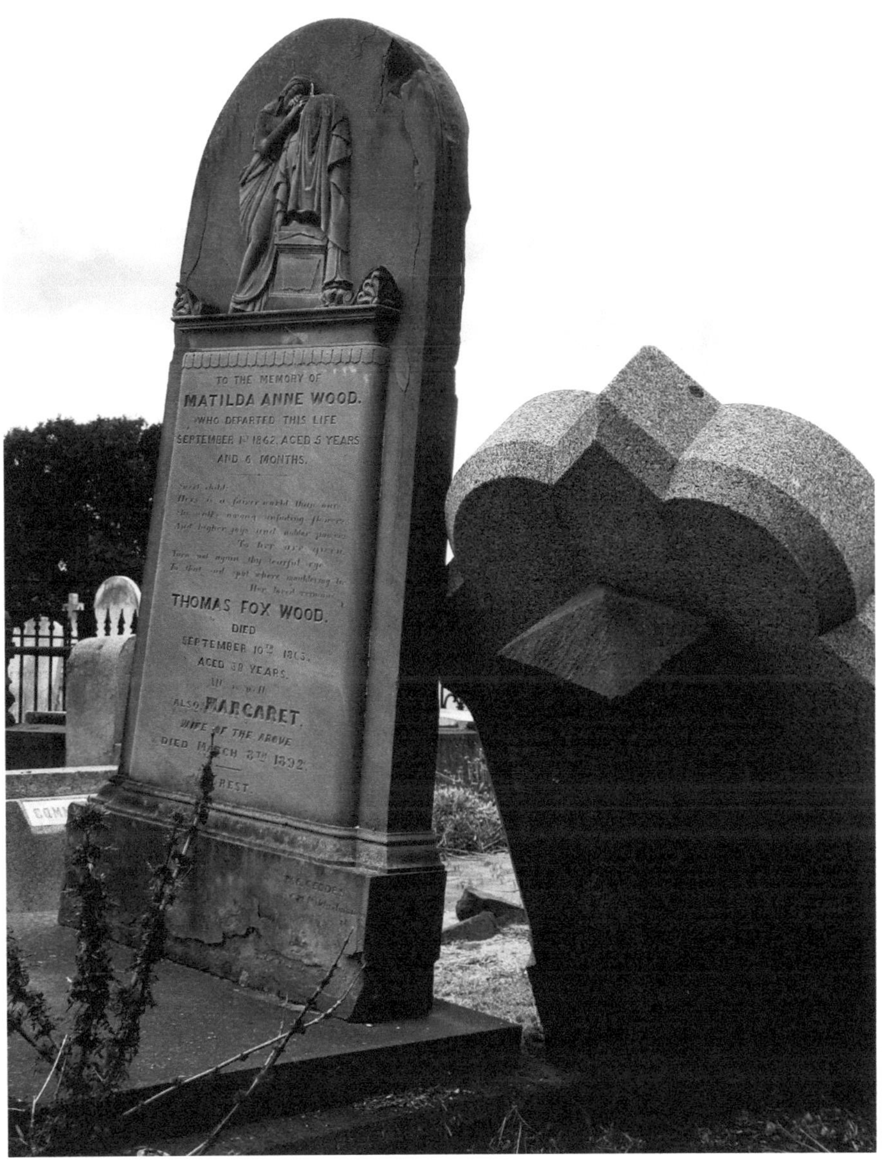
TO THE MEMORY OF
MATILDA ANNE WOOD.
WHO DEPARTED THIS LIFE
SEPTEMBER 1ST 1862, AGED 5 YEARS
AND 6 MONTHS.

THOMAS FOX WOOD.
DIED
SEPTEMBER 10TH 1865,
AGED 38 YEARS.
ALSO MARGARET.
WIFE OF THE ABOVE
DIED MARCH 8TH 1892.
REST.

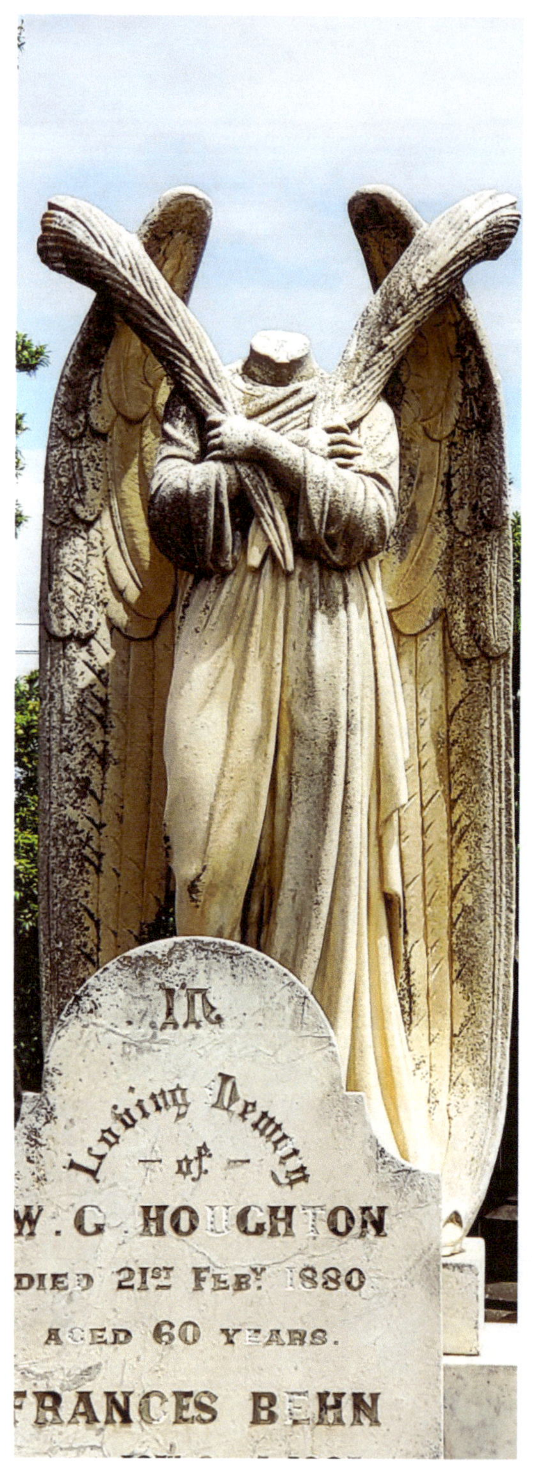
In
Loving Memory
- of -
W. G. HOUGHTON
DIED 21st Feby 1880
AGED 60 YEARS.
FRANCES BEHN

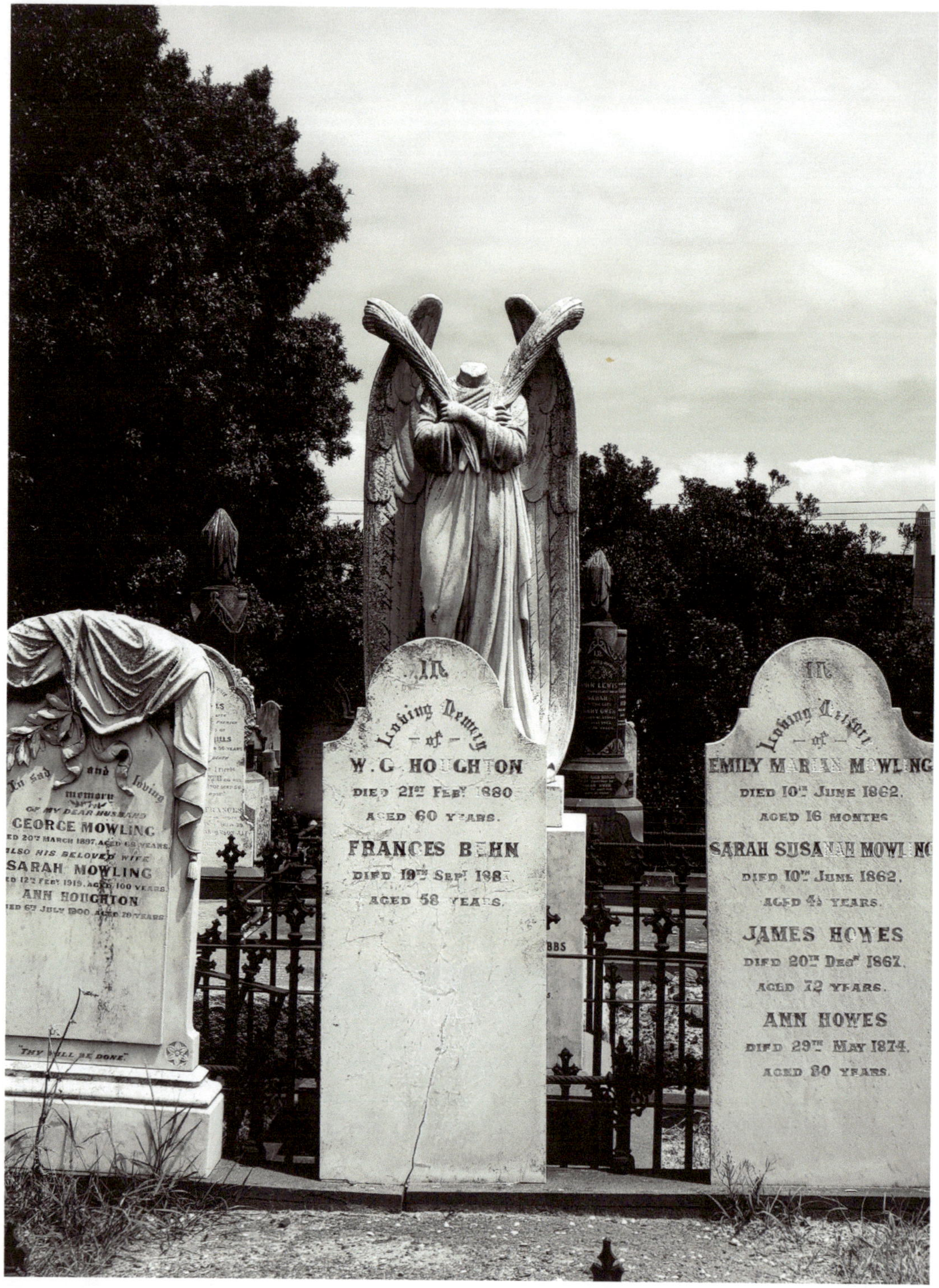

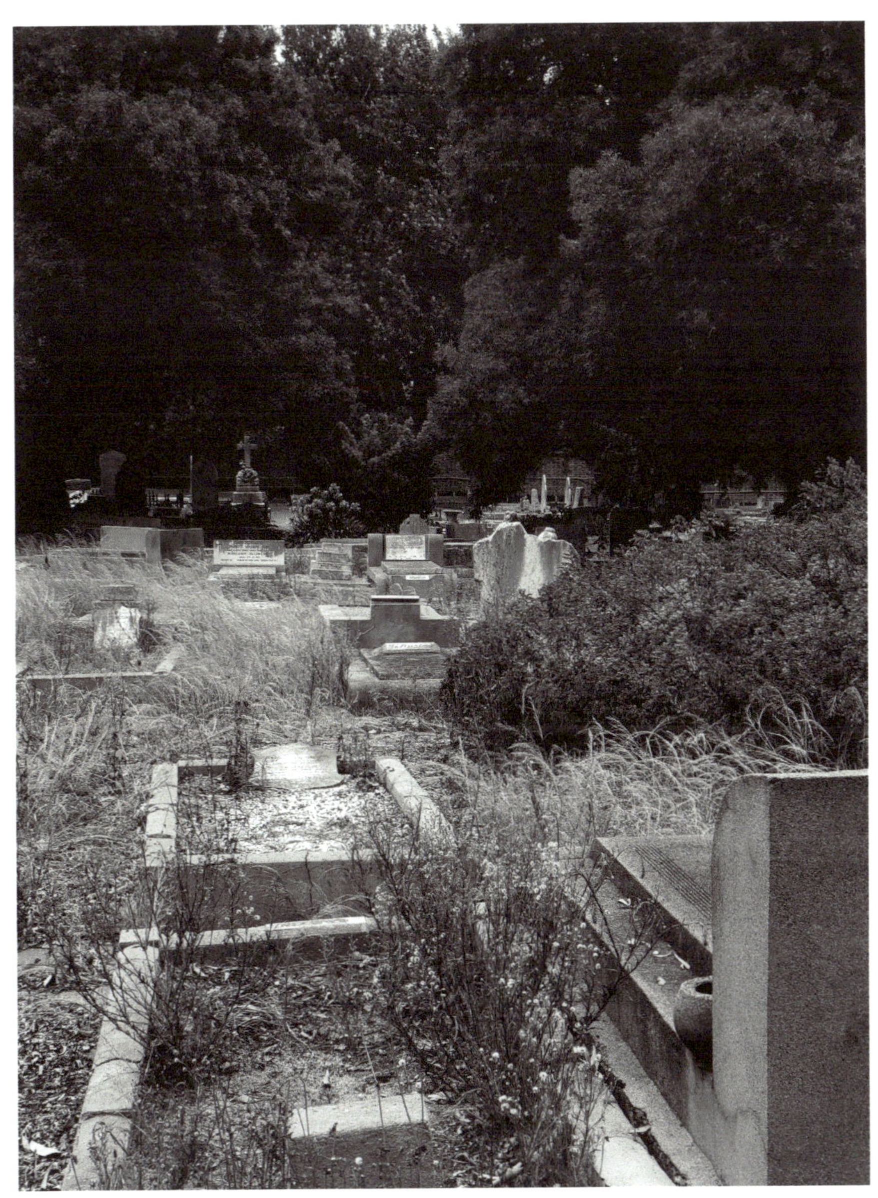

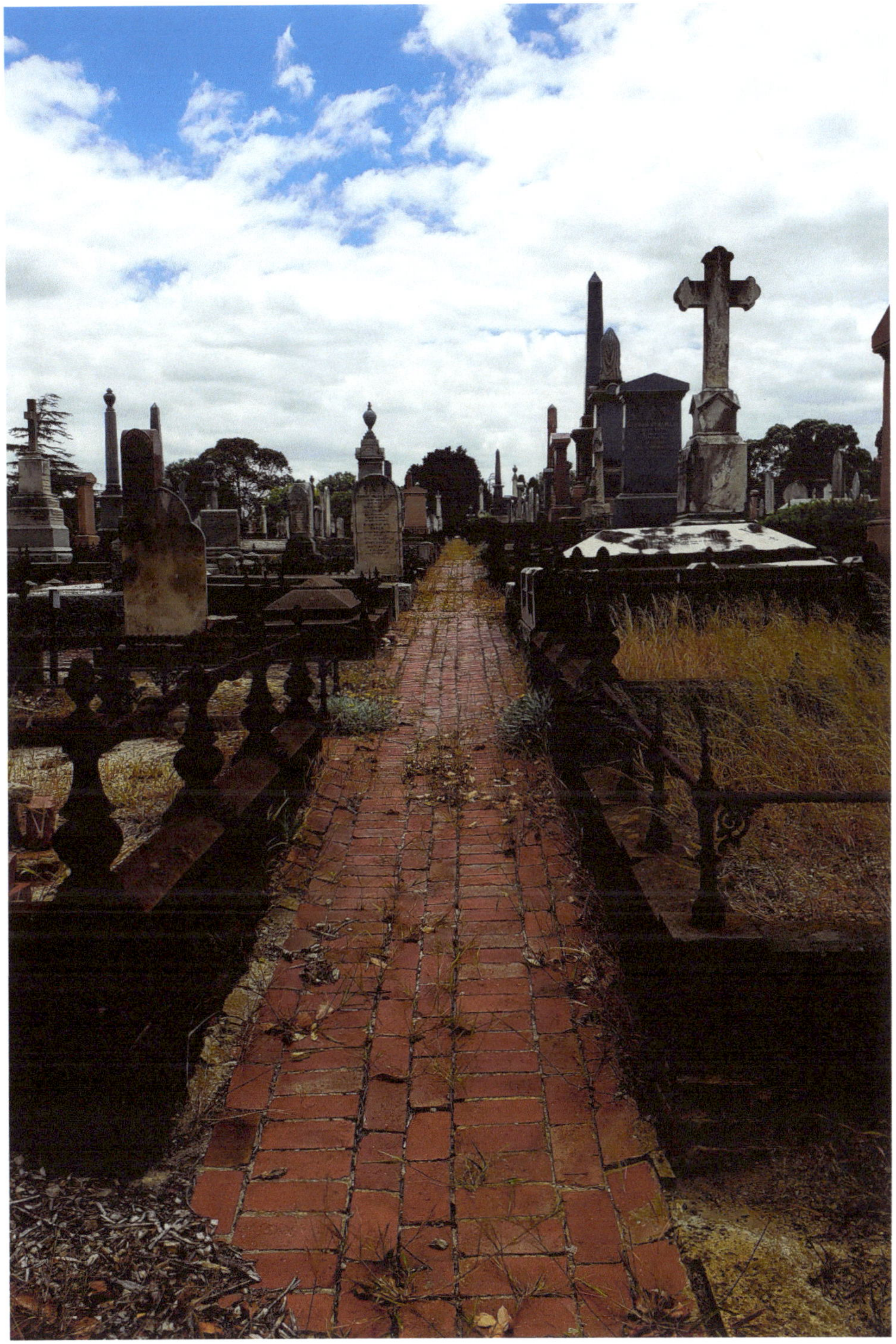

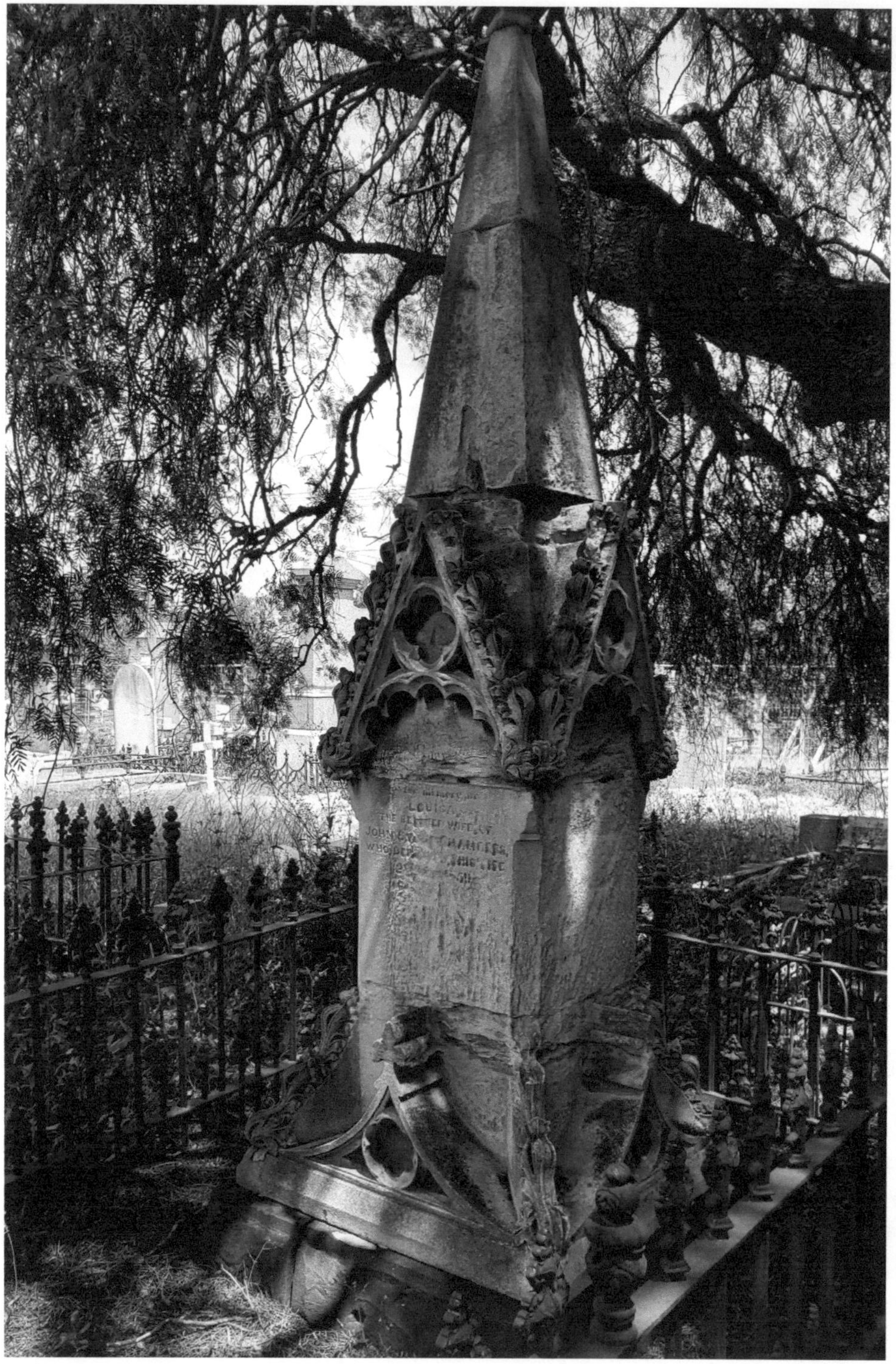

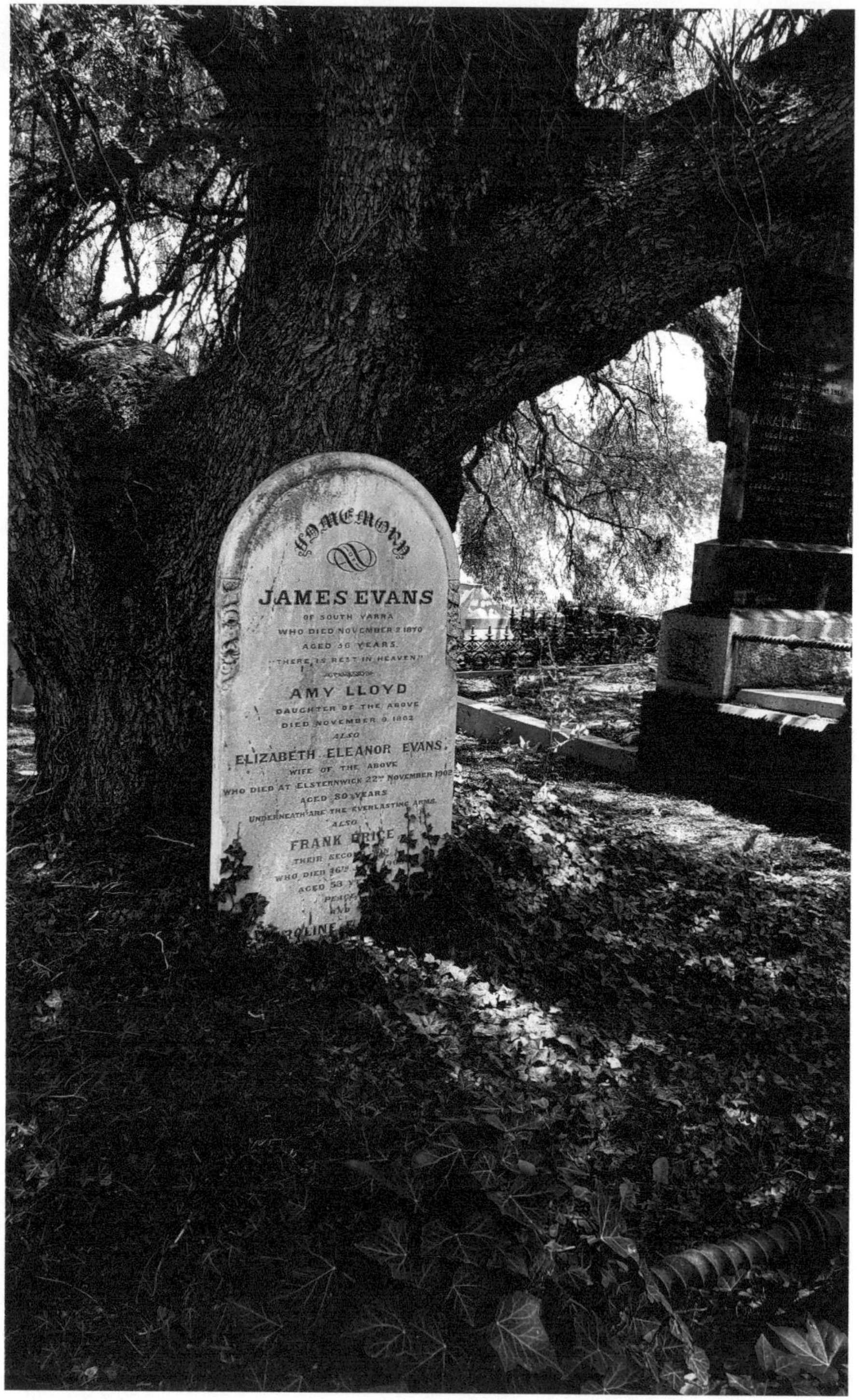

IN MEMORY
OF
JAMES EVANS
OF SOUTH YARRA
WHO DIED NOVEMBER 2 1870
AGED 36 YEARS.
"THERE IS REST IN HEAVEN"
AMY LLOYD
DAUGHTER OF THE ABOVE
DIED NOVEMBER 9 1862
ALSO
ELIZABETH ELEANOR EVANS.
WIFE OF THE ABOVE
WHO DIED AT ELSTERNWICK 22ND NOVEMBER 1902
AGED 80 YEARS
UNDERNEATH ARE THE EVERLASTING ARMS.
ALSO
FRANK PRICE
THEIR SECOND SON
WHO DIED 16TH
AGED 53 Y
PEACE
CAROLINE

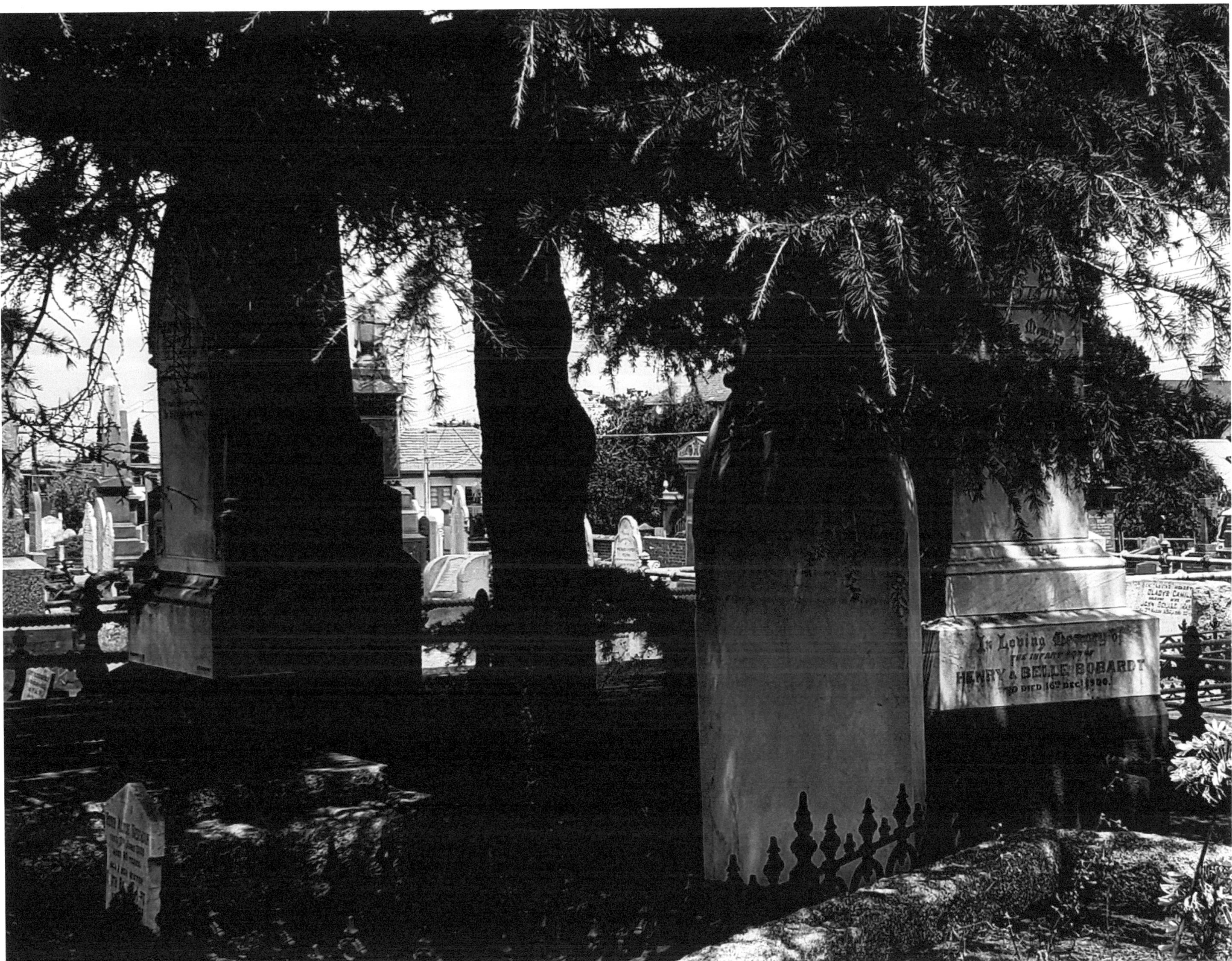
In Loving Memory of
THE INFANT SON OF
HENRY & BELLE BOBARDT
WHO DIED 16TH DEC 1900

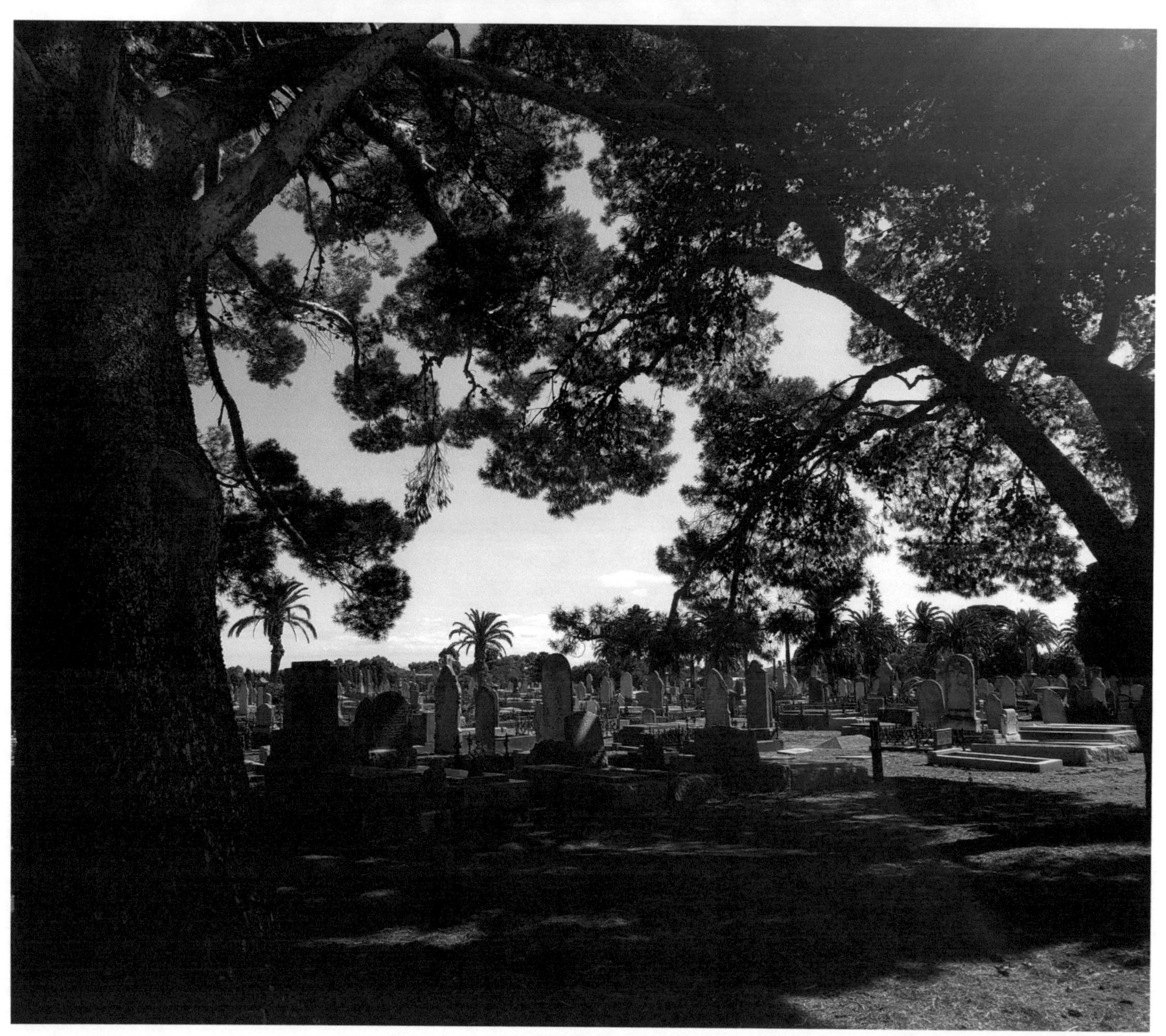
Williamstown Cemetery

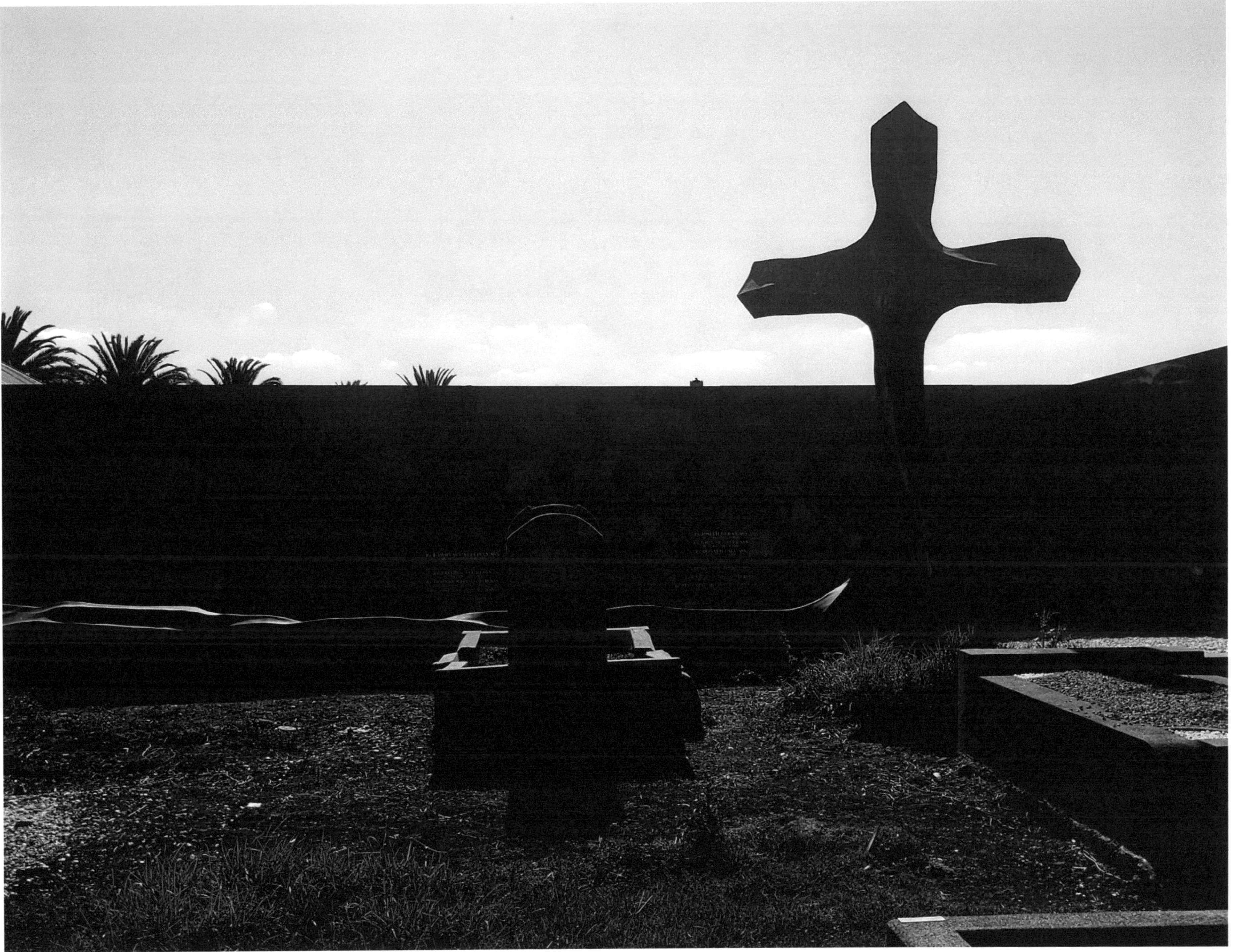

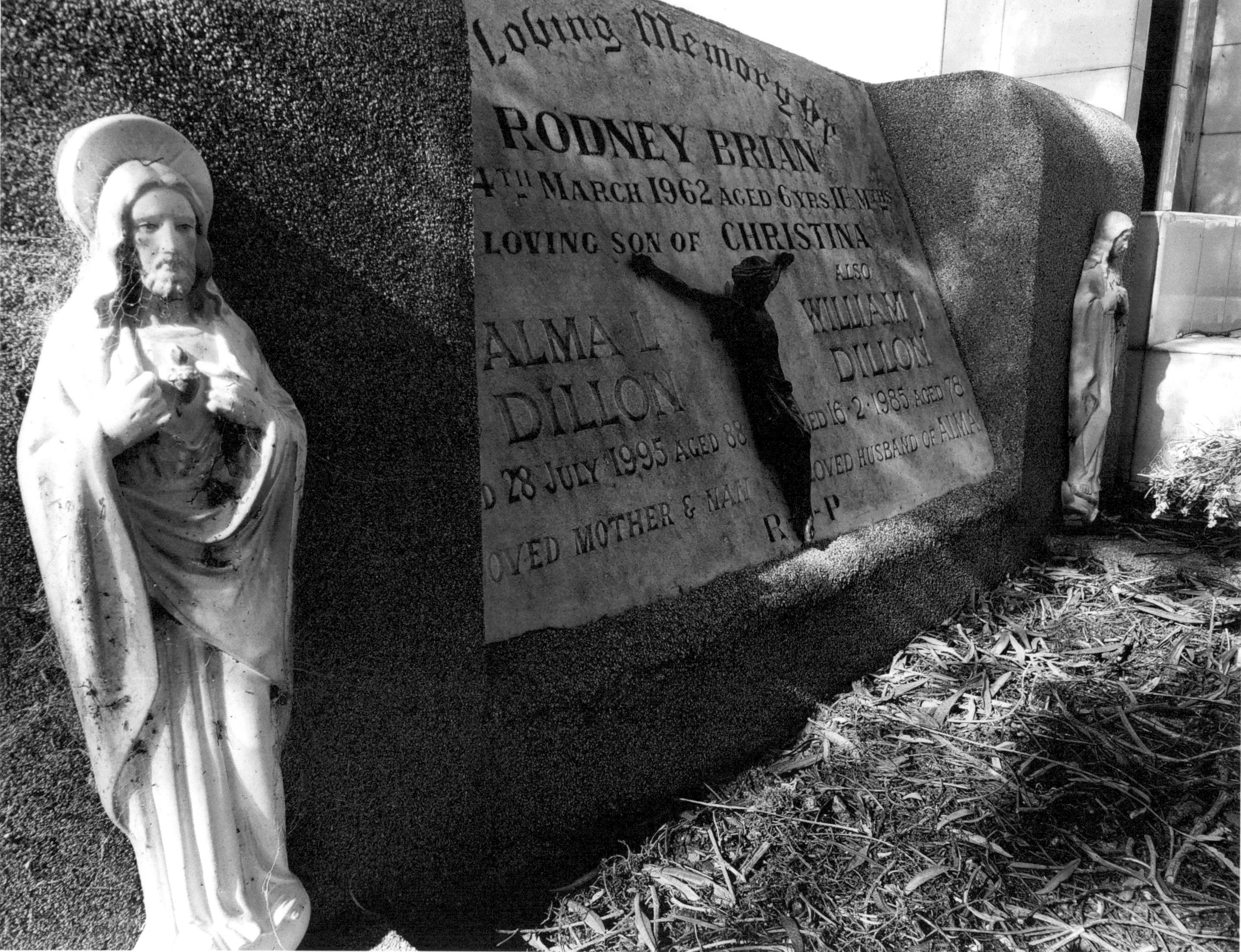
Loving Memory of
RODNEY BRIAN
4TH MARCH 1962 AGED 6YRS 11 MTHS
LOVING SON OF CHRISTINA
ALMA L
DILLON
28 JULY 1995 AGED 88
LOVED MOTHER & NAN
ALSO
WILLIAM J
DILLON
16·2·1985 AGED 78
LOVED HUSBAND OF ALMA
R·I·P

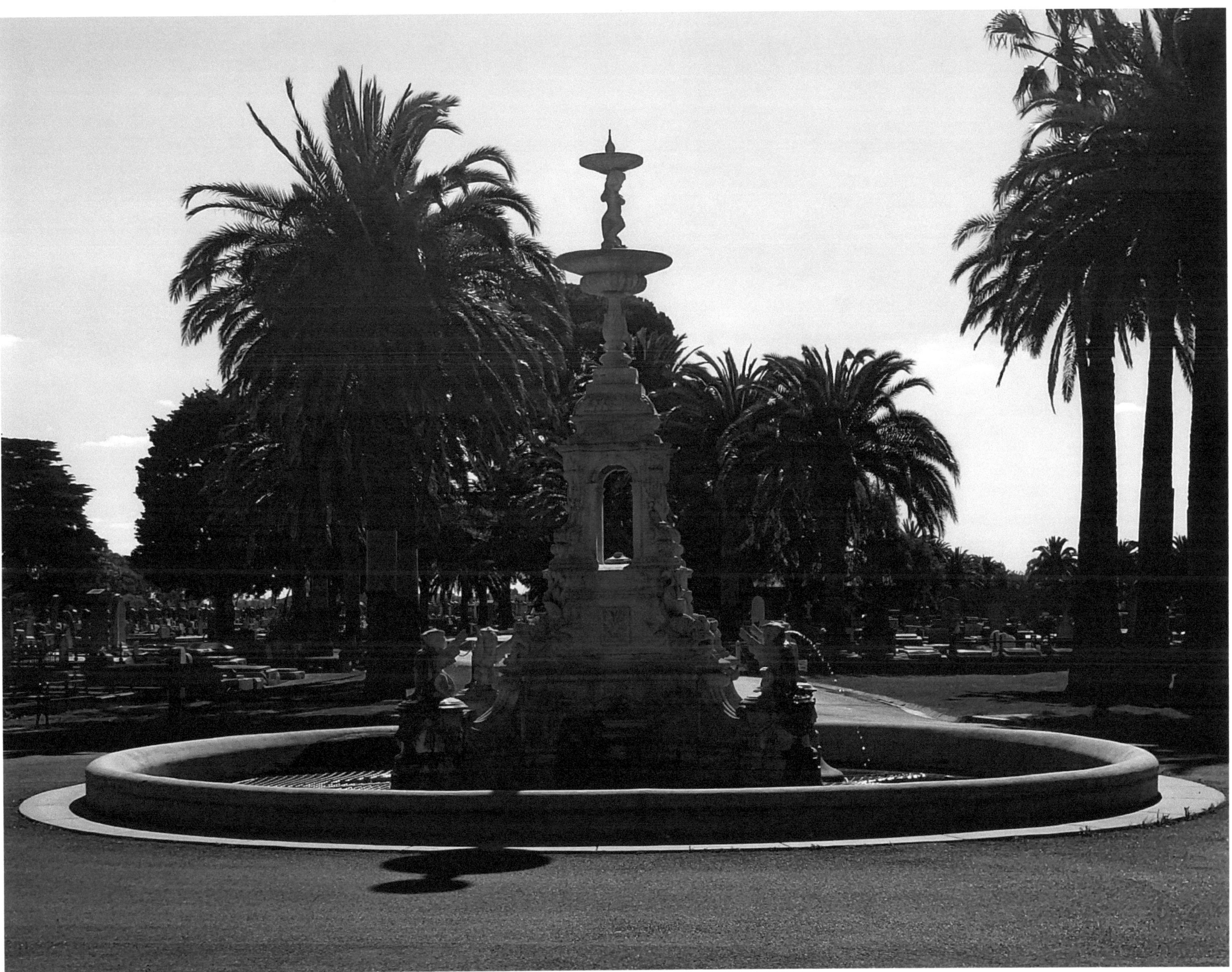

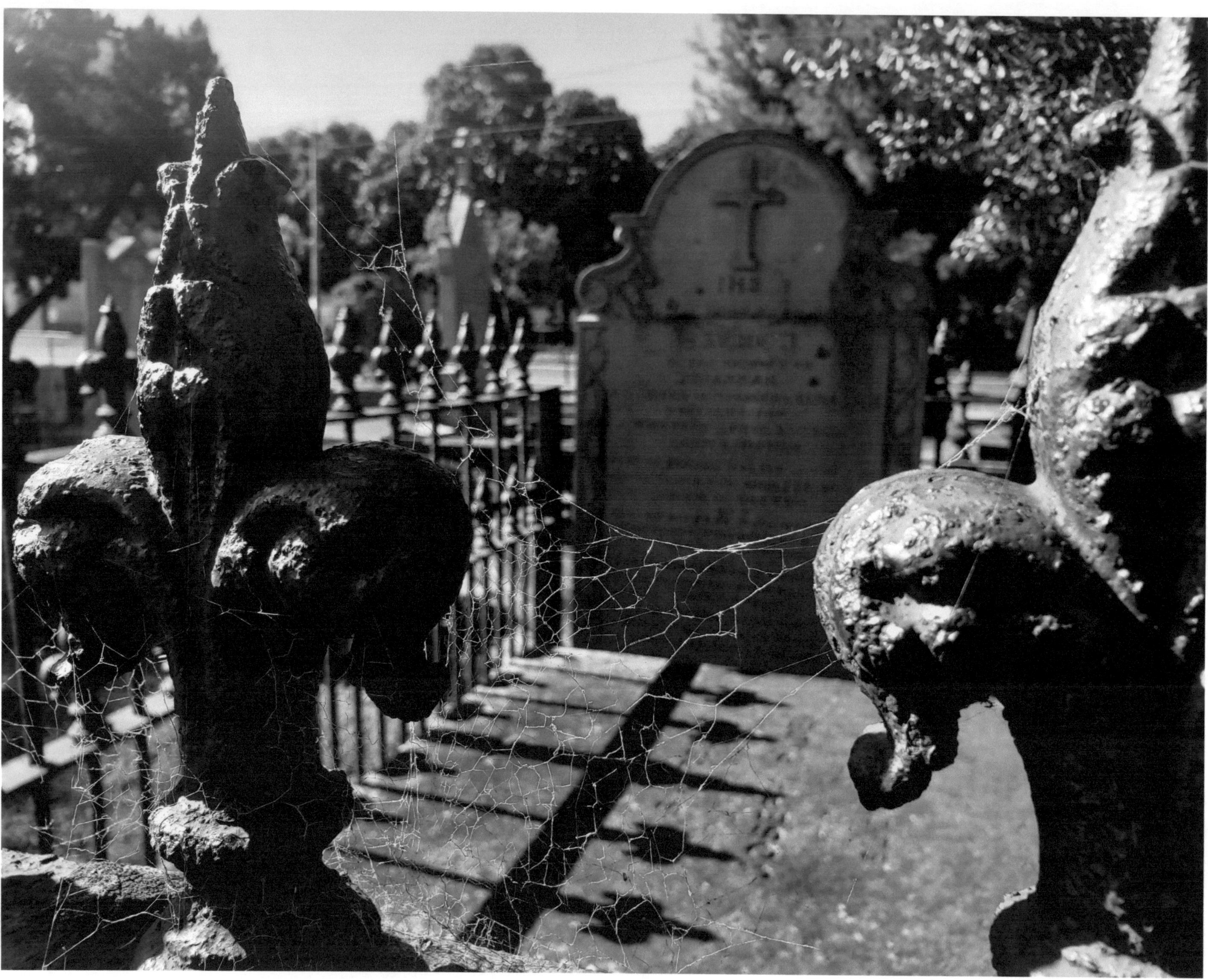

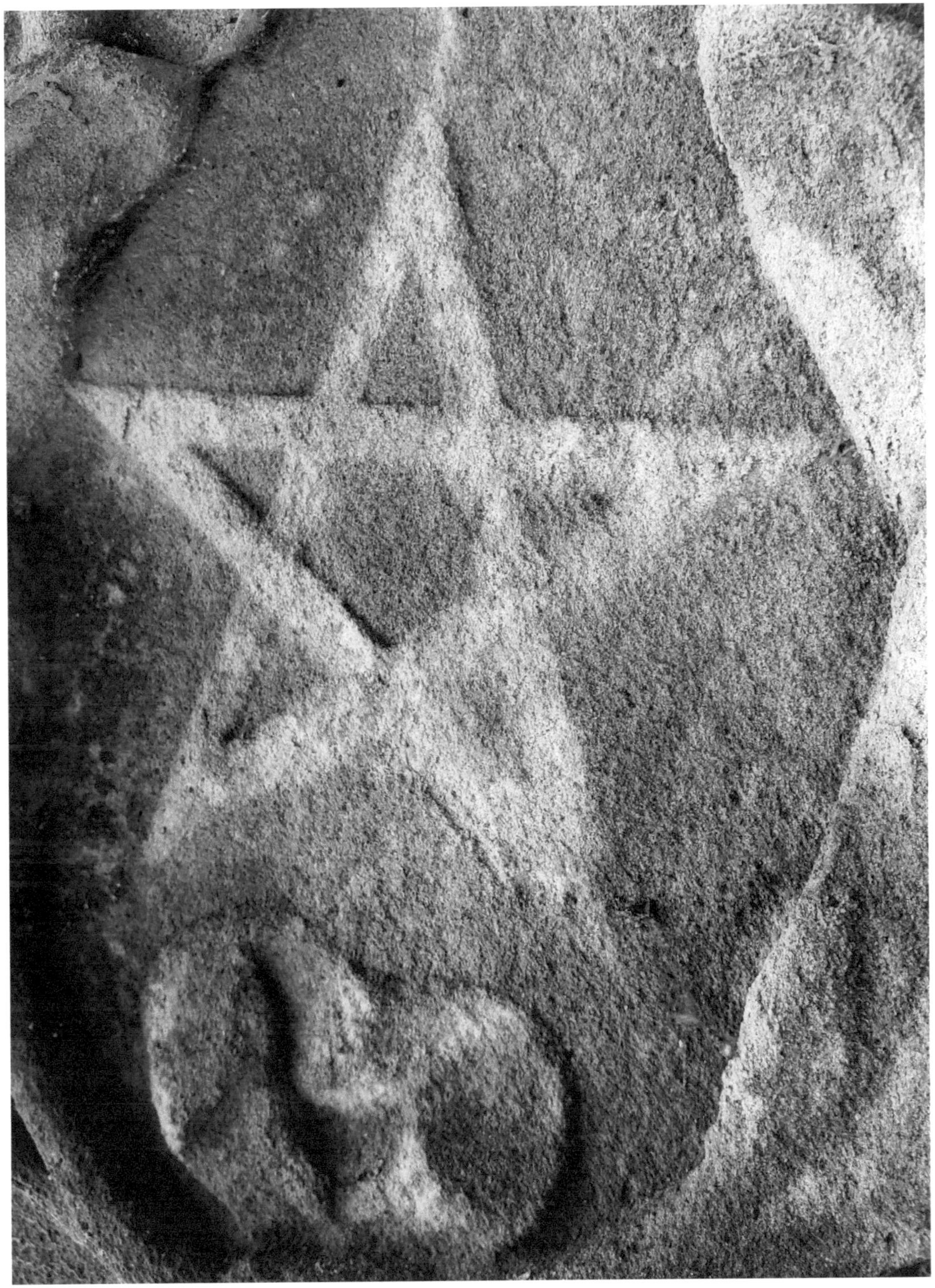

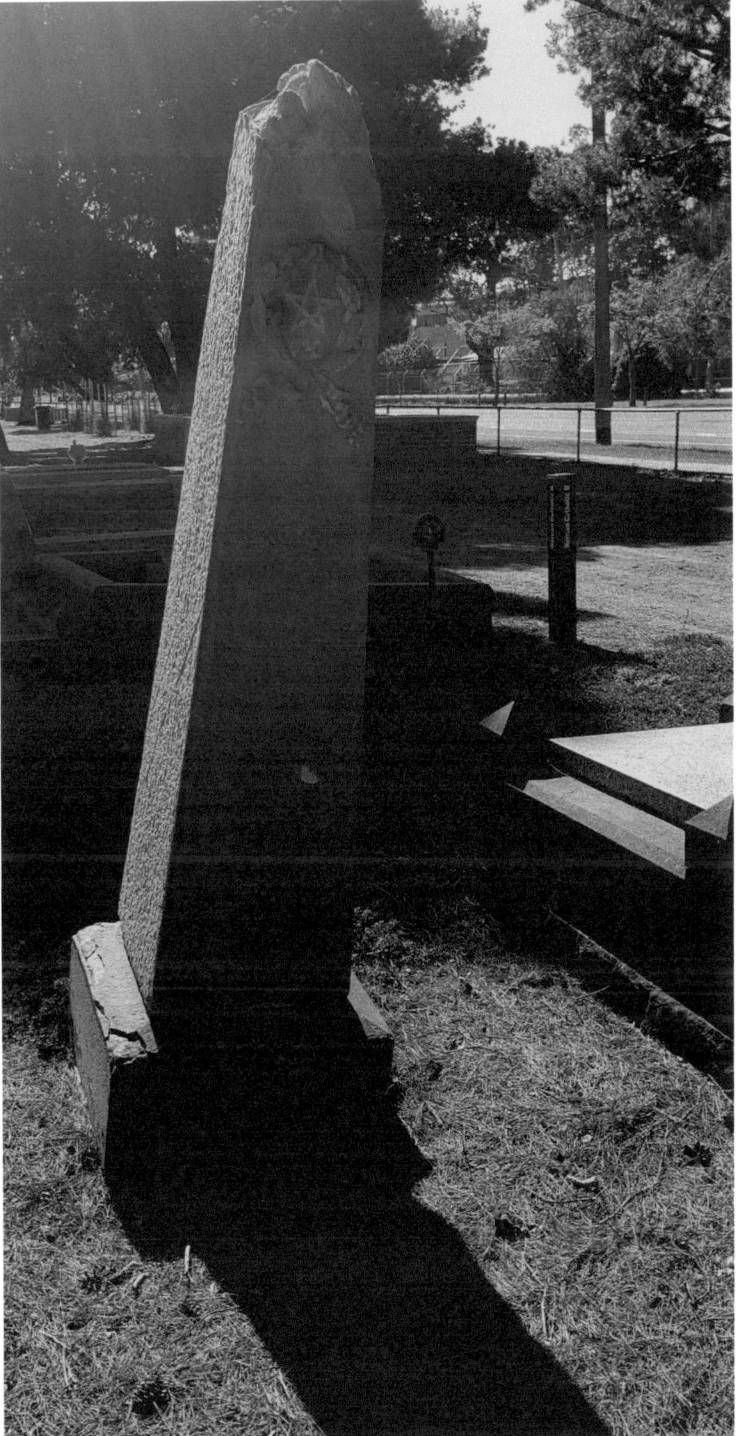

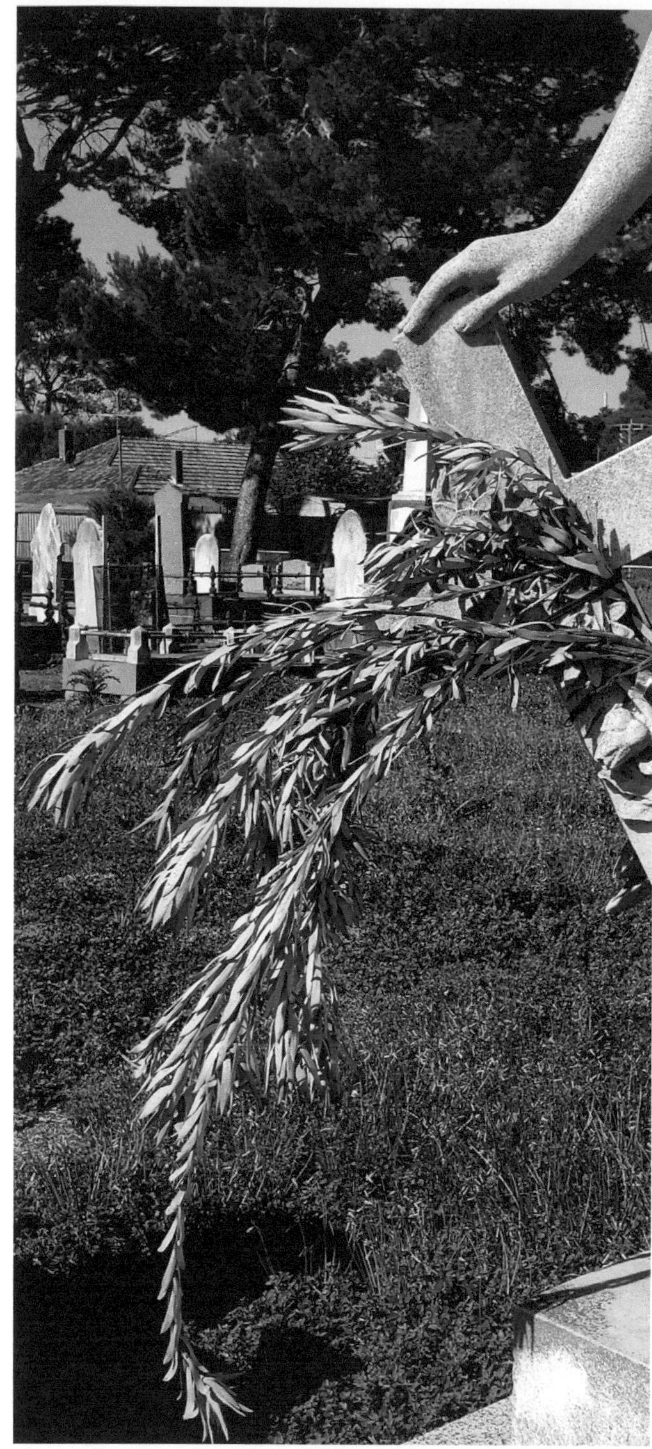
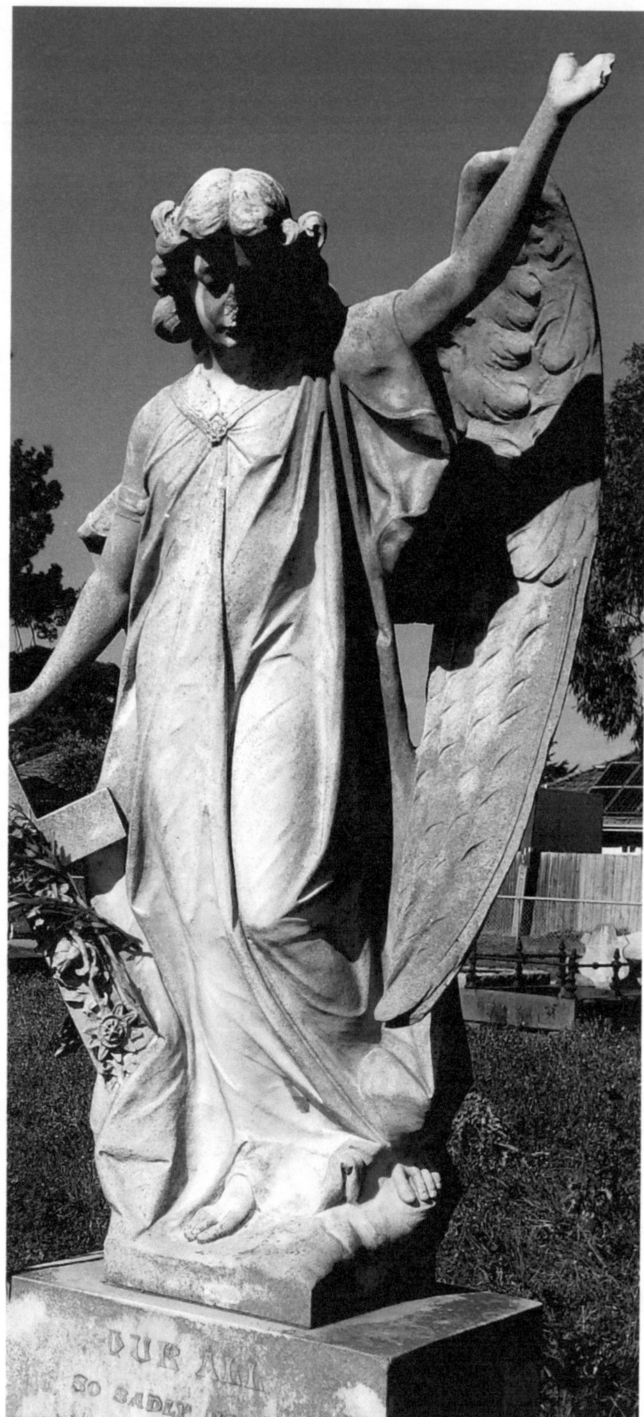
OUR AM
SO SADLY MISSED
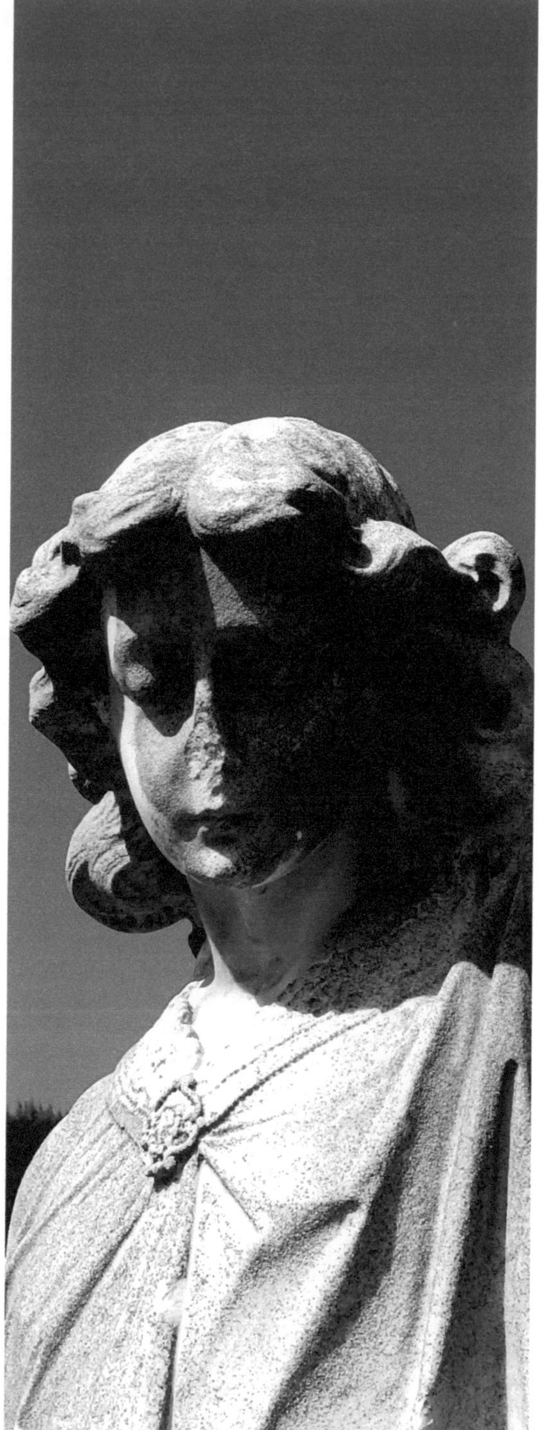

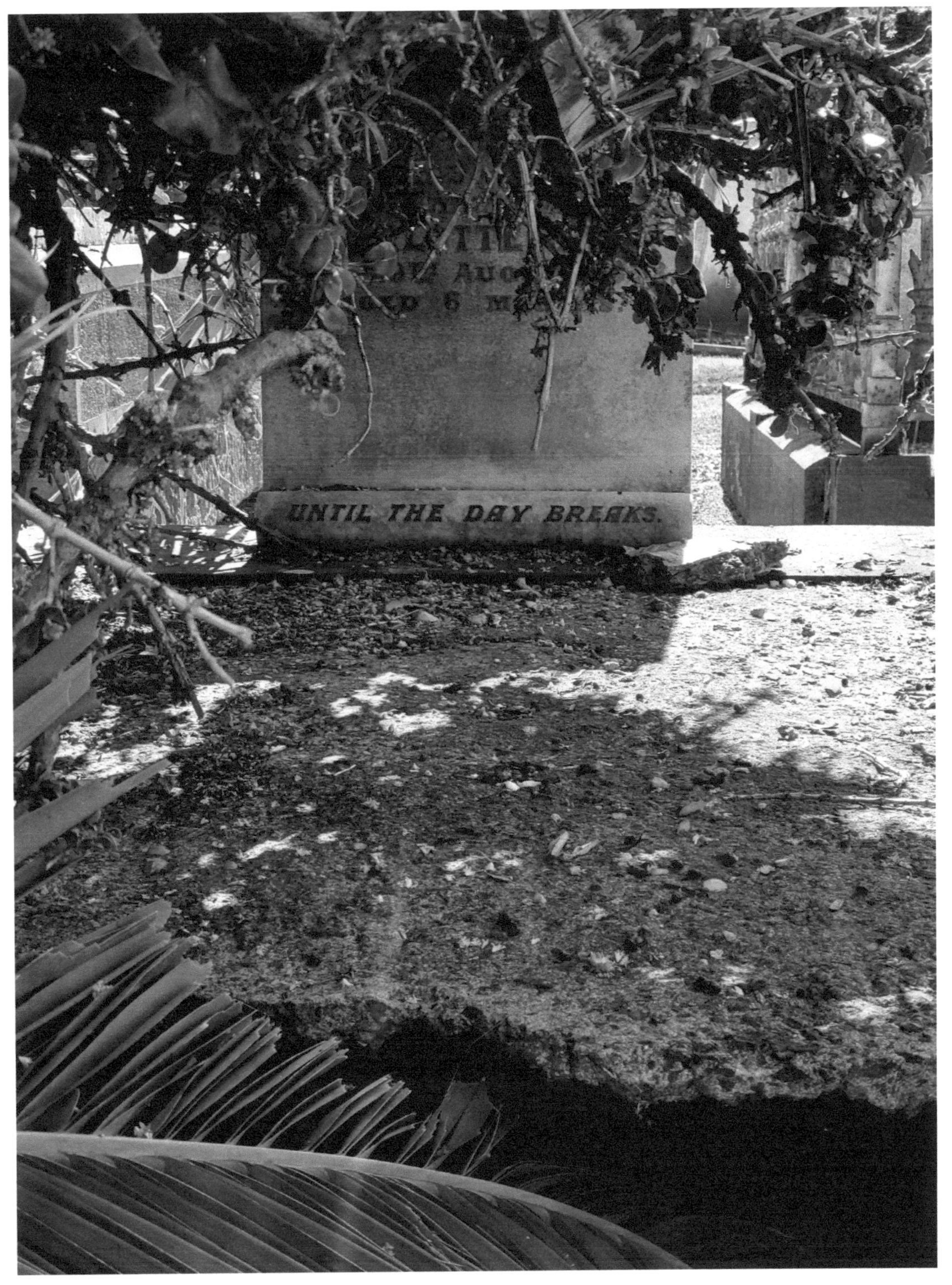
UNTIL THE DAY BREAKS.

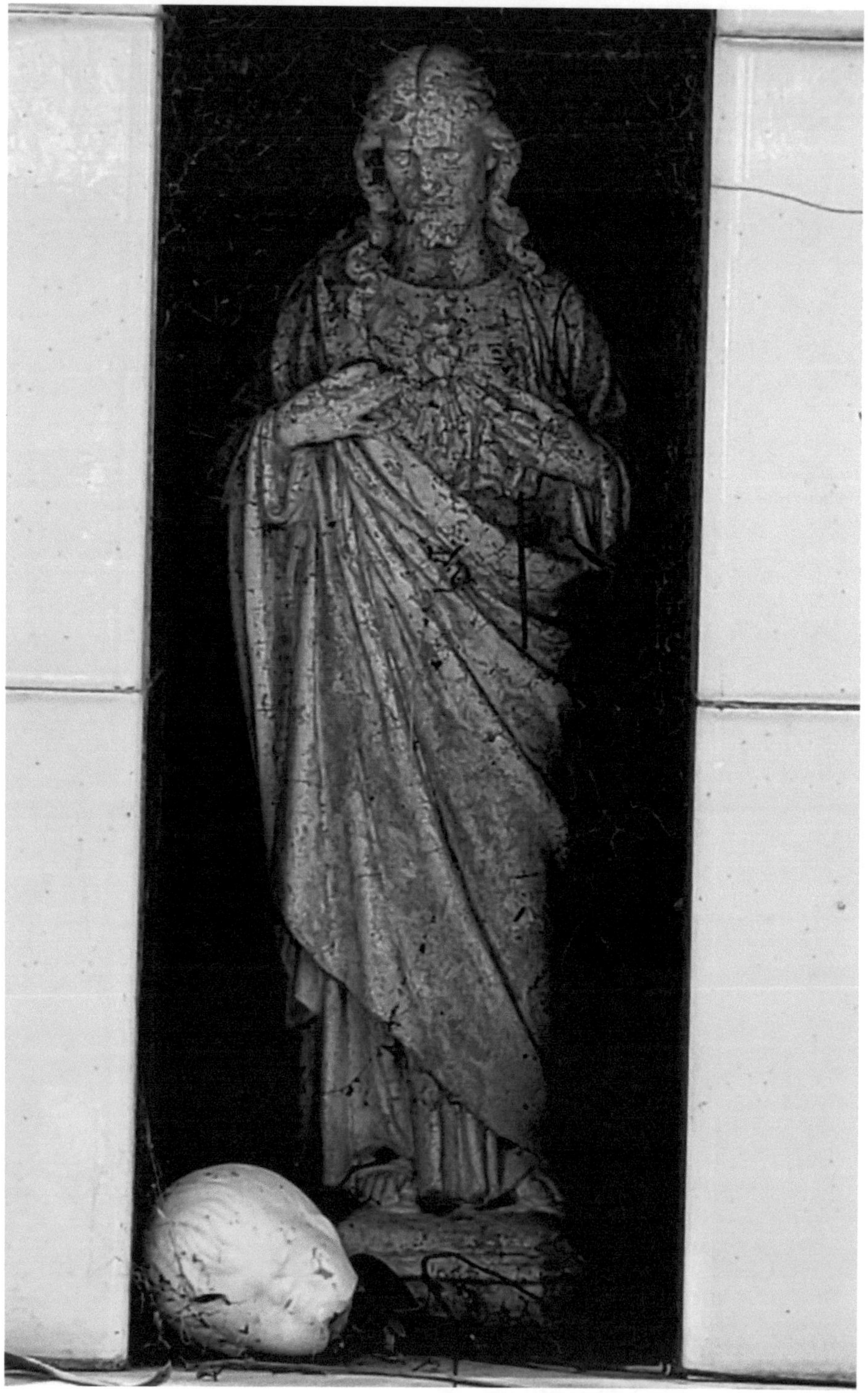

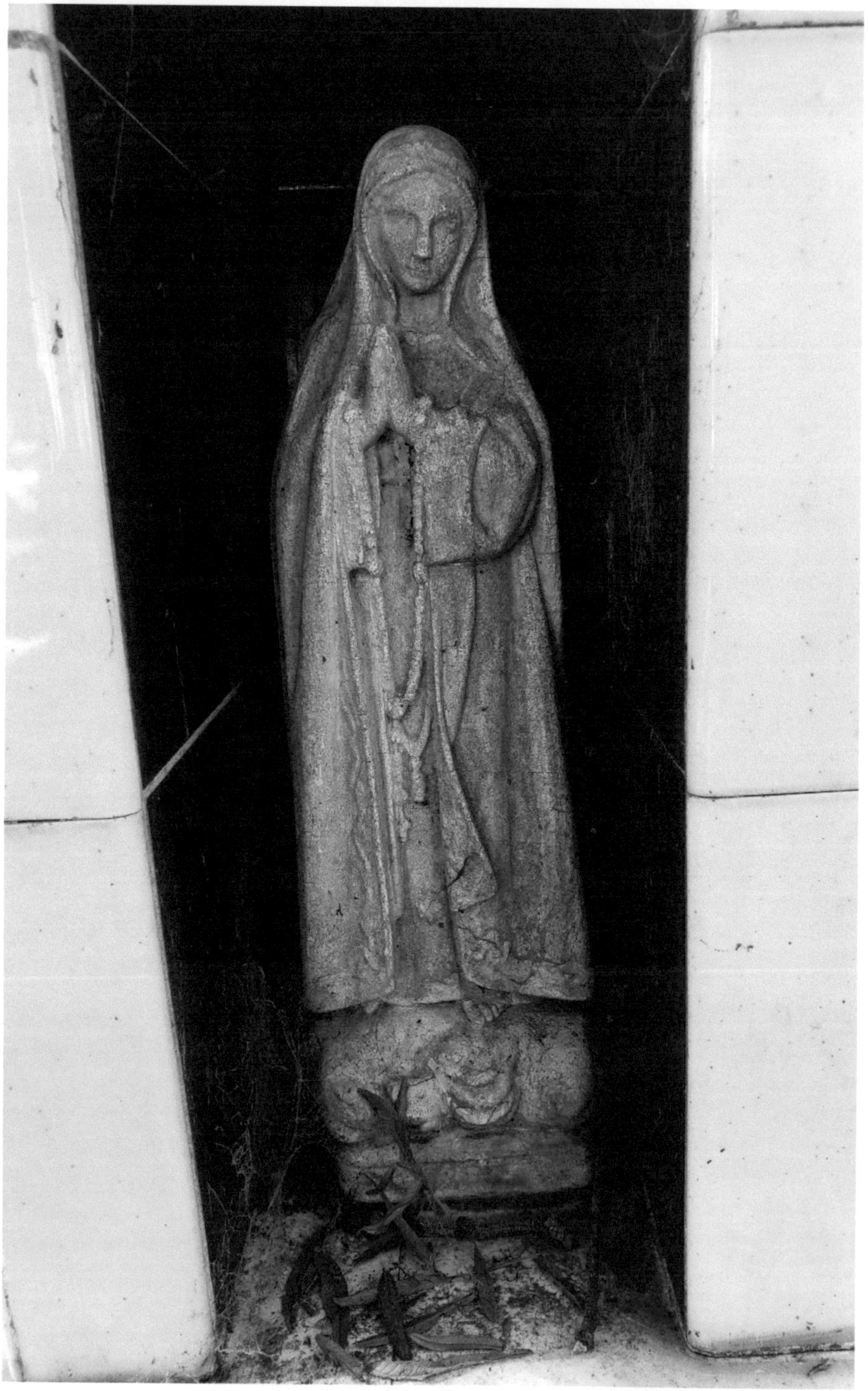

About the author

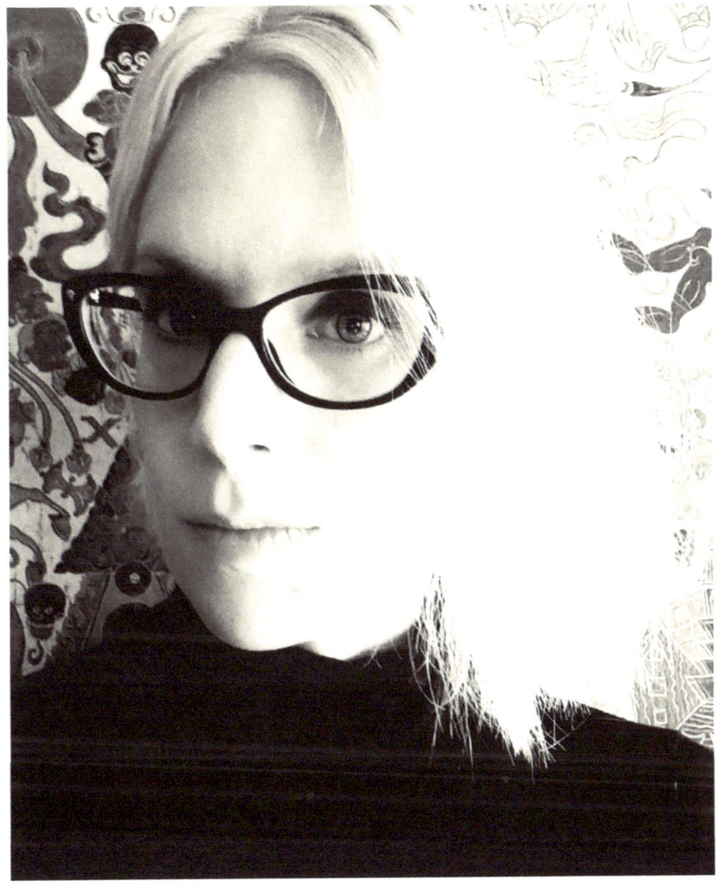

Elizabeth Bedlam a Michigan Native, lives and writes from Melbourne, AU

She has been featured in anthologies and zines that you have probably never heard of:
Anti-This/Anti-That,
Low Life,
Horror Sleaze Trash,
and Soiled Purity

Her most-read works include

"Hello Old Friend"
and

"The Way The Light Falls."

She has been praised for her realistic depictions of neurotic females

Instagram: @elizabeth.bedlam or @swann.bedlam

Correspond!

Email: elizabethbedlam@gmail.com

Website: swannbedlam.com

9 780645 958607